Steelhead & the Floating Line

A MEDITATION

Bob Arnold

Illustrations by Loren Smith

Frank
Amato
PORTLAND

Dedication

For my mentors, Lee Wulff and Ken McLeod. May there be steelhead where you've gone.

"The aspens are changing, their leaves are turning to Guinea gold, precious, priceless, privateer plunder," said the old woodcutter. "Now there's a hue that defies all painters, a tone reserved for October's brush, not to be counterfeited by man. Changing aspens set the mood of October and only October may paint them."

"What I am about to tell you is not about the changing aspens; it is about the native steelhead arriving daily. The females, their cheeks lightly burnished with the violet of sunlight shot through a prism, bearing cargoes consigned to the creation of a new generation. The males losing the silvery sheen of the sea, tarnished by the time away from tidewater, spectrum-streaked and looking as sunshine seen through distant rain; in their bodies, too, gifts for that new generation. All native steelhead bring their bounty of life-giving beaded genetic jewels; treasures kept in trust since the beginning of terrestial time."

—Alec Jackson, "October"

My special thanks to Alec Jackson, who read this book in manuscript and made many useful suggestions. Also, he shot all the fly plates with his trusty Nikon.

Cover: Author's fishing flies, made with found materials.

Published in 1995 by Frank Amato Publications, Inc.
P.O. Box 82112, Portland, Oregon 97282
(503) 653-8108
ISBN: 1-57188-040-2
UPC: 0-66066-00231-3
Illustrations by Loren Smith
Book Design: Charlie Clifford
Printed in U.S.A.
1 3 5 7 9 10 8 6 4 2

CONTENTS

imitations—Dry-fly design (2)—Some generic configurations—Use of the hair stacker—Curt's fox-squirrel fly—Tying Royal Wulff—Natural flies vs. attractors—Some textbook exercises—A long, eventless afternoon

Wild steelhead, about to be released.

ONE

At a certain time of the year, a river can be said to "go over" to the dry fly. Exactly when this is is subject to debate. Roderick Haig-Brown said it was when the water temperature reached 55 degrees F. and the air temperature was warmer than the water. (This ideal temperature was quoted earlier in the *Hardy Angler's Guide for 1923* and is attributed to A.H.E. Wood.) It is a good rule of thumb, though by no means an absolute. It may come earlier or later. On my river, the North Fork of the Stillaguamish in Washington state, various people believe it to arrive at different times. And this will change from year to year, depending on conditions. Generally, though, it is when the river has rid itself of much of its snow runoff and is settling down nicely into a pool/riffle configuration again, with a discernible current entering a pool and running down its center and fanning out over a boulder-strewn bottom. The river will be showing an exciting shade of green and the tops of the rocks will be visible, even in runs that are six feet deep.

Each year I keep asking dedicated fly fishers when they think the river is ripe for the floating line and fly. Each year I keep getting an original answer. George McLeod (who knows a thing or two) says it is towards the end of July, and he doesn't get serious about it until August. Guide Mike Kinney believes it is way earlier, and I am inclined to agree with him. Depending on the year, it may be at the end of June. Surely throughout July and most definitely all during August and September. And Walt Johnson—whom I perhaps wrongly accused of fishing sunk line into August, some years—now fishes dry fly whenever he ventures out in summer, declining the early wet-fly season.

And me? Well, I'll waffle on this. I am inclined to start later than I should, and miss out on some good fishing. This is because I am a wet-fly fisher at heart, and love the challenge of covering a deep, long pool through the traditional method of step-fishing, casting long and letting the line form its belly and proceed to swing through the pool, fishing all the water thoroughly—well, at least the water on my side, for a wet fly behaves oddly on the far side of the river, hanging there indecisively and then whipping madly down into the channel and not beginning to fish well until it is about mid-point across the river. Thus, a wet-fly fisher covers only those fish on his side. Often this is a small percentage of the steelhead in a pool. He gets his strikes mainly from fish that have taken up odd positions, ones moving about and lying in temporary resting places in just the right places to intercept his fly. Often these are fish he has disturbed earlier by entering the water.

Not so with the floating line and fly. They behave very differently and for effectiveness require a steelhead that has settled down and begun to adapt to the river environment. Ordinarily this happens after the fish has been in the river for a while, which coincides with when the river has undergone its seasonal drop. But I'm told there are a few rivers where a fish just out of the saltchuck will respond immediately to a floating fly or one fished in the greased-line fashion. The fish is thought to recall its two-year period in the river as a juvenile, when it fed voraciously and competitively for every morsel the current brought within striking distance, for there is not much food in the rivers on the western slope of the Cascades. It is slim pickings and in order to survive a fish must be aggressive.

It is believed that the steelhead—both juvenile and adult—is the most pugnacious of the salmonids, and I would agree, based on what I've read and observed about their life in the river and at sea. They are known to bully every other species and to give no ground. I used to spend hours watching this year's hatch in first the slack water, then in the shallow riffles, and the degree to which they dominate their river environment and command everything within reach is awesome.

Once I stunned a deer fly that was attacking me and dropped the still-fluttering insect on the edge of a backwater rivulet that had very young steelhead in it—they were no more than a couple of months old and only slightly longer than an inch. Sure enough, soon one baby steelhead, then another, peeled out of formation and began to try to drag the struggling insect—bigger than themselves—by its legs under water, where I suppose they proposed to eat it.

Of course they couldn't submerge it, but this didn't stop them from trying, until the current grabbed the fly and whisked it away, with them pursuing like tiny piranha.

TWO

Fishing with the floating line is so incredibly pleasant that I always wonder why I didn't start earlier in the season. One reason is my love of wet-fly fishing, but another is because there is often a wide period of transition when both methods are equally deadly. This is why anglers like myself foolishly persist with a method that has lost its effectiveness until the lesson is driven into our pig heads by some overt act that cannot be ignored. This year it was Errol McWirt's catching a twelve-pound hatchery fish on a no-name floating fly and teaching us all a lesson. By us all I mean George McLeod and myself and Errol's partner, Jack Sandstrom. It happened this way.

It was barely summer and the year was one in which (for a change) we had some sustained snow runoff that kept the river happily high throughout June. Errol and Jack fish a marathon day, as though engaged in some fierce competition to see who can stay on his feet the longest. They start out on a weekend day by driving to the North Fork from Bellingham early enough to arrive before first light. And then they fish until dark. Naturally there are times during mid-morning and late afternoon when to do what they are doing seems insane even to them and they slow down, and since they are gregarious, they often find themselves stopped by a riffle and chatting away in the sun with whomever comes along and acts friendly.

Though I try to avoid fishing weekends, I sometimes find myself doing just that. It was late morning when I ran into the pair. Eleven o'clock on this year's crowded Sunday morning usually gave me a fish, so I kept coming back. They had begun fishing upstream, as usual, as soon as it was light enough to put one foot in front of the other; they had been fishing wet—they showed me their five-foot sink tip lines. Even though the sinking portion was short, it was made from one of the new miracle materials with a density beyond belief. It got down to the bottom in a wink. Errol had a factory-made one, but Jack had fashioned his own and had interchangeable tips of various lengths. They had flogged the upstream water all the way from Fortson to well below Seapost, with not a hit to show for it.

I had arrived late at the Manure Spreader Hole, which looked to be high but showed a wonderful configuration. This fine pool varies greatly from year to year. It is recipient of the greatest burden of silt from the infamous DeForest Creek slide up on Deer Creek, and in some recent years has been naught but a shallow, sandy pool of shortened length. This year it had a stony throat, widened sweetly as it did long ago into the start of a deep, lengthy run, and contained an attractive gut running down its center a little towards the far bank. Its only drawback was that it looked pretty sandy until you got to the end, the tailout in front of Bill Street's old place, and then the rocks began to appear in good numbers, though most were close to the near bank where you waded.

Already I had taken a number of fish from this fine pool on sunk line. Most were remnants of the Deer Creek run of wild steelhead, with the odd hatchery fish mixed in. But now—at the end of July—things were slowing down. This late Sunday morning I found the pool newly unoccupied, which was a hopeful sign. I always fish a pool that has no anglers in it or on its bank as though I were the first person through it that day, even when I know I'm not. So I covered it as I had been doing, sunk, but no fish came to my fly, and when I reached the bottom I snagged a sucker. As I released it and prepared to leave, I saw Errol and Jack coming down the beach from where they had crossed the Deer Creek riffle. We hailed each other and compared notes. Meanwhile, George McLeod was encamped with his family and grandchildren on his property a couple hundred feet down the beach. I left.

What happened next I was informed about the following week. The two men began to fish the pool with the same fast-sinking lines they had been using upstream. But halfway down, Errol, who was following Jack, decided to try something different. I think it was more for the sake of variety than from any sustained belief in the efficacy of the dry fly. He stopped, went ashore, and changed reels and lines. He experienced no action (dry-fly fishing is mostly like this, aside from piddlers coming out and drowning the fly) until he got near the bottom of the pool. Then a fine fish—one that had seen my cleverly fished wet, plus Jack's—rose to the dry and sucked it in.

The steelhead promptly went into action, was duly played out, and landed downstream a short distance—right in front of George's camp, as a matter of fact. Now George believes he practically invented dry-fly fishing for steelhead, which is not true, but he did invent Purple Peril, a superb dry fly.

And he is good at it. He thought dry-fly fishing time had not yet arrived on our river. Another week or ten days, yes. Now his eyes told him otherwise.

And—after hearing from Errol about his feat, the following Sunday—how did I fish for the rest of the day? Why, wet, of course. Even looking at the river, a bit lower than a week ago, I still didn't believe the time was right for dry.

What time is, then? It is always sooner than you think.

THREE

A floating line is so much fun that it is a wonder anybody chooses to fish any other way. (The response is obvious: it is to catch more fish, which a sunk line does, most of the year.) A floating line allows every inch of water to be covered, not just the pockets and pools that are wide and deep enough for a fly to sink, swing, and straighten out. On my silt-plagued North Fork good wet-fly pools are few and far between. It takes a mile-long walk to take you from one to the next, and what you find often proves disappointing—a run that you can cover in two wet-fly casts, and then it is on to the next pool, another mile's walk away.

Fishing a floating line allows the angler to investigate tiny guts and streamlets and lies that are the size of a bathtub. Not to mention riffle water, with its good cover, high oxygen content, and stony bottom—all characteristics of excellent steelhead-holding water. And you can fish tight to a shady bank, which is another place steelhead like to lie, especially during mid-day, when the sun is high and without mercy.

A dry-fly line is a joy to cast. A long history of thought and design has gone into the manufacture of today's lines. In most parts of the country (but not the Pacific Northwest), anglers fish floating line once spring has arrived, and they keep at it until a cold snap and rain or snow has changed the river's characteristics; we persist with sinkers here.

More and more now my reel spools contain floating lines, and even my sinking lines are floating ones with about 24-feet of tip cut off and pocketed so that I can fish a wet-fly tip. I like the way such a line handles—the way it feels in my hands, when I gather in coils in preparation for the next cast. So it is easy for me to loop back on the floating head and have restored my full floater, even while in mid-current. (The interlocking loops are far enough out through the guides not to be annoying or have to be stripped in through the tiptop before making my next cast.)

I like a rocket taper, a line that is essentially a double-taper floater for forty-plus feet, before it shrinks its diameter and becomes a shooting or running line. This gives me the best of both worlds, for I can mend much of the back portion without moving my fly (or moving it very much; if you riffle or wake a fly, it doesn't make much difference whether you move it a bit or not) and also a line that will shoot an impressive distance. It is satisfying to watch a good fly caster with such a line reach "fine and far off." On the Wenatchee, down from the upper Monitor bridge, each year I see some skillful angler casting distances that I'm sure I cannot achieve.

How graceful it is to see your own or somebody else's line sail back, form its bow, and then come arching forward again to place its fly some eighty or ninety feet away. Of course to catch trout (and many steelhead) you don't have to cast very far, so exhibition casting distances are not really necessary. Dry-fly steelheaders are inclined to cast too far, most of the time. It is a carryover from wet-fly fishing and reflects a desire not only to reach the far bank but to extend the drift and swing of the fly, thereby covering more water and increasing the chances of hooking a fish. When fishing a floating line, steelheaders have to keep reminding themselves not to cast so far. Often fish can be caught right at your feet. This is especially true if you are standing on the beach, not out in the water.

On my river, below Deer Creek, there is a long tradition of fishing dry from the beach, or close to it. It is so strong that the McLeod clan fishes dry with hip boots. George, following the lead of his dad, Ken, urges this. The hippers are a reminder not to wade deep. The reason is simple. A fisher standing in the water disturbs the fish. A little summer steelheading drives home this point. Fish are easily spooked.

Early this season, I made my annual visit to Fortson. I knew there were fish in the pool, but they quickly become sophisticated and don't get caught often. The pool is bounded by an ancient riprap left over from days when a railroad spur used to run to Darrington and bring back timber from Summit Mill. The rocks are imported and huge, and steelhead often lie in among them in positions impossible to cover. So I fished through the pool with a light sinking line and—as I expected—hooked no fish. Nobody else was about, so I crossed the tailout and went up on the riprap to spot the pool—something I ought to do more often. I saw four nice steelhead. I wasn't surprised. What astonished me was where they were lying. Mostly it was over sand. This is not supposed to happen.

George McLeod

Two lay near the rocks in the impossible to hook positions I suspected they would be in. But another was near mid-river, closer to the side I had fished from than I would have imagined. And the fourth fish lay *behind* where I had been wading only a couple of minutes ago. Now, I know for a certainty that none of those fish would have been lying in most of those locations if anybody had been in the water. The fish would not have left the pool, but they would have moved as far away as they could from him and taken up positions where the rocks on the bottom and the rocky outcropping of the riprap would protect them.

The amazing thing was the short length of time it took the fish to resume new stations once I was out of the water. Provisionally I concluded:

step into a pool, no matter how big or how quietly you do so, and the whole environment of the pool and its fish changes substantially. Some fish may actually flee and seek out new water; they will probably barrel upstream, past you, and head for the broken water at the head of the pool. This is more likely than them going downstream to the run below. But more probably they will subtly change their lies in the pool you have entered. And after you have stood still for a while, they may actually resume some of their old stations. They will be aware of you occupying their watery world, and they will behave differently from before.

I'm not saying they won't strike, after a period of time. Often they will. Perhaps they choose to disregard you and go on with their lives, or else they forget about you. (A steelhead doesn't have a very big brain and not much resident memory.) But the river environment will have changed, and the difference will be to your disadvantage.

The old North Fork anglers used to stand on the beach and cast into the near water for their steelhead. And often, if they were the first on the water on a given morning, a fish would take right at their feet. This was generally in broken water of about the same depth that a wading wet-fly fisherman starts feeling comfortable in and where he begins to lengthen out his casts in blithe anticipation of a hit.

How often we wet-fly fishers must send fish scurrying when we stride boldly into a pool, as if we own it. (We may own it for the time being, but surely we don't own its fish, all of which we have probably "put down" for ourselves and others.) In mid-summer an early morning wet-fly fisher (and they nearly all are) will eliminate his only chance for the day's fish by such a careless, hasty act. Think of it: the early rising, the breakfast in the all-night diner, the suiting-up in the dark, the long walk in blackness to the pool—all canceled out by one quick misstep.

The traditional North Fork dry-fly fishers used stripping baskets—those quaint little belly buckets that usually testify to the user's inability to handle coils of line. The stripping basket permits the long drift of a wet or dry fly because the thin running line can be fed out of the basket to any distance the length of the pool requires. On the Flat Water and in the center of the Manure Spreader Hole this was a long, long ways. And on the Columbia and its tributaries, such as the bars of the Snake, the effective distance for such a drift was near endless.

Of course the fly dragged; drag couldn't be avoided. And if it couldn't be avoided, it had to be turned to one's advantage. I'm not sure where the idea of intentionally dragging a fly got started but I think I know how.

FOUR

Trout fishers believe a dragging fly won't get a rise from any self-respecting fish; hence, they do everything possible to prevent it. Of course it is impossible. The only way to avoid drag on a dry fly is to cut it off your leader and flick it off your thumb out onto the surface of the water. If you do this, you'll find the fly behaves most unlike any fly you've ever fished. For one thing, it will turn in circles in the tiniest of back eddies or at the place where two currents come together. One is always moving faster than the other and the difference (or differential) is what causes the whirling effect.

A fly tied to a leader, no matter how fine, behaves as though attached to something. Now the fish might not care. Steelhead seem to like this being-attached quality. They are more likely to be provoked into attacking something than being fooled into thinking something is really food, for which they have no nutritional use. It has to do with the fly moving faster than the speed of the current over a long distance. Hence, if you can't avoid drag, even with a directly upstream cast and gathering line—quickly, quickly—back into your hand as it comes racing towards you, why not turn the drag to your advantage and make it work for you?

How do I fish a dragging fly? Glad you asked. As much like an F-7 Flatfish as I can.

What?

Yes, there is a certain bob-and-weave a boxer has and a wiggling plug comes close to imitating, when it is doing its best work. The fly (or trolled Flatfish) wiggles a bit, nearly stops, starts again, stops again, twitches, bobs, flinches, dips, and finally goes under, as drag becomes too great in most types of water. The fly struggles. It is not unlike that little bird, the sandpiper, that is always crying, "Help, oh help. I'm crippled. I'm trying to escape, but I can't get away from you." The programmed bird is actually trying to take you in the opposite direction from its nest. But I think many times the bird has no nest, no eggs, no fledglings, and is performing its little act for no worthwhile purpose. It is part of its program—produced by its microchip.

I like my dragging fly to come as close to that fluttering action as possible. The fly is intended to dominate the pool with its action and tell the steelhead, "Oh, please, don't come out and strike me. I'll be gone in a minute. I'm just trying to stay alive."

And the steelhead says, "Sure, you bet. I've gotten to be this considerable size by taking the likes of you at face value. Proceed, friend. But first, gulp."

And you've got him.

Lee Wulff once told me that Royal Coachman, or Royal Wulff (a fly he nicknamed "Strawberries and Cream"), was such an effective fly because it looked unlike anything a trout had ever seen. But it looked tasty. The trout would "reason" that it was not going to get a second chance for something as luscious as strawberries and cream, and it had better seize it before another trout did. This manner of thinking is how trout get big and also explains how we get acquainted with them on the end of our line.

A dragging fly should dominate the pool. Every fish lying in the run ought to be aware of it and have to make the conscious decision *not* to pursue it. This is its wisest course, since a steelhead is not hungry at this stage in its life. But your hope is that there is some steelhead around that is a sucker and won't be able to resist something so buggy and sexy. It will nail it for the same reason that Herschel the sea lion—already fed to satiety on steelhead and salmon at the Ballard Locks—will attack yet another fish and take a bite that he does not intend to swallow. We'll call that reason "for fun," for lack of any better word to describe it, but it is a wanton act, and one that can be manipulated for our gain.

FIVE

W hat is dry-fly fishing? Must the fly remain on the surface? At all times? During all, or only during part of its drift?

During the publication of my book, *Steelhead Water*, it became necessary for my editor/publisher and me to talk on the phone frequently. This was difficult, for we were both always off fishing different water. I think a man who writes fishing books and articles ought to fish a lot, whether or not he catches many fish. Likewise an editor or publisher of fishing books. If neither of them does, well, they are assuredly in the business, but I have reservations about them as persons and as fishers.

Frank and I always began our conversations with inquiries into how our respective fishing was going. We were polite; that is, he listened to me go on and I listened to him go on. What mattered most to each of us, of course, was talking about our own fishing. And it was possible that one or the other of us might let drop some clue that would help the other know where to go to fish next or to do better where he was currently fishing. This was partly why we listened so raptly to each other.

It was August, and Frank had not done too well on the Deschutes yet, or else he had and was keeping it from me, which did not seem to make any sense, for I don't fish that river. The only other reason might be from force of habit in not giving anything away. I am a suspicious type, especially about fishing reports. For instance, I know fishers who lie about not catching fish. They will nail a steelhead or two, and when you ask them how it is going they will tell you sadly they are not doing any good. I don't think Frank is like this, though I can't be sure.

So I asked him about his latest trip to the Deschutes. "I had fair fishing," he admitted. Fair, it turned out, was hooking fifteen fish in three days. That is better than fair; it is superlative fishing. I asked what flies were taking them and how he fished them.

"Mainly the Orange Bomber," he told me keenly. That is a waking surface fly, with a big snout of calf hair to make it plane in the water and a clipped deer-hair body to keep it afloat.

"All on the surface?" I inquired.

"About thirty percent," he offered.

"And the rest?" I persisted.

"Wet," he explained.

"How wet?" I prodded.

"In the first inch of the surface."

I whistled. This was fun fishing, no doubt. The question now arises, was this dry-fly fishing? If it isn't, I think it comes close enough to count. And it offers a good definition. If you catch your fish in the first one-inch of the surface, it is for my purposes dry-fly fishing. It is dry because "true" dry flies often sink to this low level of wetness inadvertently during the course of their drift and so are unable to be differentiated from other floating or riffling or waking flies. If a wet fly is fished dead drift so shallowly it ought to count for something, something important. It is part of that family of flies all fished a little differently but manipulated on a floating line, and this is what I will be talking about in this book.

Alec Jackson, who read this book in typescript at my request, protests here. He argues that if a fly is fished in the first inch of surface water, it is by definition greased-line fishing. In fact, A.H.E. Wood preferred his flies fished "awash" in the first half-inch, Alec says.

I think we do not disagree so much as agree to quibble. What we are after is effective fly fishing and ways to have exciting fun. The fact that a full floating line is used exclusively is what links us, now and in times past.

Alec Jackson

SIX

I wander around a lot, I know, and I skirt some issues. Bear with me. We will cover all the pertinent ground in time. We will get there when we arrive. Of course there is a bit of Zen Buddhism in all of this. Catch-and-release fishing for wild summer steelhead on a floating line and a fly that does peculiar things on or near the surface is not for somebody without a metaphysical bent or for one who wants to bring home a lot of meat. It is for a person who has a lot of time to kill in a manner he believes to be interesting, difficult, and meaningful. Most of all, it is for one who loves being on a river during the warm time of the year.

Back in the old days when nothing but wild steelhead populated our rivers (there being no successful hatchery programs, but no real need for them, either, for there was no massive environmental degradation from logging, etc., to require salmonid bolstering), the Canadian Bob Taylor used to spend August on the North Fork fishing dry fly. He was regularly employed and this was his main vacation. He fished the mile of water directly below Deer Creek and sometimes a little bit more, if the inclination moved him and it was not too hot.

He averaged one bona fide steelhead rise per day. It was enough. How many fish did he land in a week? Sometimes only one. It was enough.

I greatly admired his dedication, but did not do likewise. I thought I could do better, fishing wet. Sometimes I did, but often I didn't. Then I became a half-hearted convert.

(I never said it was going to be easy, did I?)

We generally fished dead-drift dry fly. We fished it as we did for trout, trying to keep drag at a minimum. We tried to make our flies behave like natural insects and draw no more attention to themselves than, say, a caddis or tiny mayfly might cause in the surface film.

Wrong, wrong.

We should have fished big flies like we would F-7 Flatfish, I now believe. We avoided many steelhead that would strike no other way. To put this differently, we attracted mainly those fish that were fastidious and dainty takers. These were often small fish that hadn't gone to sea for long and were used to their dinners of small insects in a recent river setting. Plus we attracted every parr in the river.

What we should have done was goad those fish, lying supine in their warm pools, into striking. We should have challenged them with meat sandwiches, instead of offering them hors d'oeuvres. When I think of all the hours we wasted with our subtlety and indirection, I wince.

I was fishing with Chris Crabtree last summer. We kept running into each other on the same pools. One afternoon we arrived at the Manure Spreader Hole at about the same time and preceded to fish it dry. When we came out of the water we compared notes. It turned out we were both offering the fish a purple dry of about the same size. I was riffling mine. The water was slow and my fly was not waking well, so its advantage was minimized.

I asked Chris if he fished riffled fly often.

"No," he said, "not really. Only at the end of the drift, when it begins to riffle naturally. Then I let it."

He asked me if I riffled mine.

"Every chance I get," I replied.

I hadn't thought of it this way before. He had crystallized my thinking. My quick reply was an indication of how strongly I believe that it should be done.

Often when the waking fly doesn't produce during its seductive bob-and-weave, it will the moment it goes under the surface. I don't know why this happens, only that it does a surprising amount of the time. It is as though the steelhead is watching all the while and is distrustful so long as the fly remains on the surface. But let drag pull it under, it now belongs to the recognizable world of the edible, or some such grouping.

As I said before, I can't explain it, only recognize it as repeatable fish behavior. This counts for a lot.

SEVEN

One afternoon a dozen years ago, I was fishing below Deer Creek in a famous pool, when Syd Glasso and Wes Drain came down the beach. I was fishing dry, they wet. Syd stopped to talk to me, while Wes went downstream to seek a steelhead in a favorite lie.

Because I had a lot of line out and I didn't want my fly to become waterlogged while we conversed (which was apt to go on for some time, since it was the first we had seen each other that year), I stripped in some slack and kept rolling my floater out into the shallows, as I stood with only my toes in the water. I had my back turned to the river so I could face Syd, which seemed the polite thing to do.

He had one of those strong Norwegian faces that seems to be unexpressive but is actually the opposite. His countenance showed a lot of emotion and, as each new subject came up, you could tell precisely how he felt about it by watching his features, which would change greatly. But if you weren't watching closely, you'd miss the show. You had to depend on your ears, instead, which wasn't so much fun, or so accurate. He was invariably outspoken, with a sharp tongue and a large vocabulary that included the profane.

He left no doubts in your mind about his opinion on a wide range of subjects.

Suddenly Syd's eyebrows shot up, his eyes became saucers. His mouth gaped.

Quickly I turned to the river and searched for my fly. Finally I found it, sodden and half sunk, as though somebody had stepped on it.

"I missed one, didn't I?" I asked.

Syd replied, "You sure as hell did!"

Knowing what had happened only seconds earlier, I tried to achieve that adrenaline rush of excitement but found I could not. It is either something that happens naturally or it doesn't happen at all. It can't be manufactured. It can't be recreated, either. My heart beat as calmly as ever and I'm sure my pulse rate was normal.

Syd, meanwhile, was all excited. He rushed away and returned, twenty minutes later, geared up for dry. Already Wes was fishing dry some distance below us. He had made the change-over all on his own by reading the water. I don't think any of us had a legitimate steelhead rise for the remainder of the afternoon.

Wes Drain fished dry—in the customary North Fork manner—out of a stripping basket, casting downstream and across, usually throwing a long line and positioning his fly close to the far bank, where it hovered for a moment, then began its zigzag, cross-stream course. I didn't see him fishing dry often, but when I did, it was always this way. He was one of the river's better fishers and accounted for a large number of fish, wet or dry.

His fly was often Boxcar, a tying of his own devise, or one of the old standards—Double-Gray Hackle, Irresistible, Rat-Faced McDougal, or Royal Coachman Buck. I don't know for a fact that he fished Purple Peril, but he would have been foolish not to.

Purple Peril started out as a wet fly, Montreal, but when George McLeod ordered claret hackles and wool from Herter's, they sent him purple. Not deterred and of a practical bent, he tied the fly with what he had been furnished and came up with a deadly dressing that has been used extensively and modified into a whole family of flies, many of them wet, including the extensive marabou series. Just look in any book of steelhead fly dressings and try to separate out all the purples. They are legion, and they are so because they are effective. They all go back to Purple Peril.

Purple Peril, however, can be improved on. It can be tied Wulff style, that is, as Purple Wulff. It is not far from that to begin with. George's Montreal-like tail of purple hackle fibers is poor in supporting the fly on the surface. Superior is gray deer-body hair, the same as the wing, or even better is purple-dyed deer-body hair. Take your pick. And the body of floss ribbed with tinsel (again, Montreal style) will not help the fly float one bit. Better use seal, or seal substitute that can be greased. Or use wool, which absorbs water to a degree, but holds the grease. The idea is to keep the fly either floating high in fast water, or riding along half-submerged in water that is slowing down.

This principle is a good one for the design of all steelhead dry flies, not just the Purple Peril, and especially for those meant to be riffled.

EIGHT

Any fly can be riffled—did you know?—including a big wet. Try it, if you don't believe me. You see? All it takes is a floating line and the riffling hitch, which is nothing more than a half-hitch or two thrown over the head of the fly. The hitch can be tied on the right, on the left, or directly below the eye, that is, dead-center. If you don't like the way the fly behaves fished one way, you can adjust or retie the hitch and make it fish another way. Or you can undo the hitch and fish the fly conventionally wet, sinking it more deeply, and riffling not one bit. All this can be accomplished with a few turns and twists of the fingers, without cutting the leader or tying on a new fly. This might be important in a run where competitive anglers are fishing close to each other and watching each other under microscopes.

A riffling hitch does not require a long leader. A short leader may be just as good or better. The degree of "standoff" between hitch, or hitches, and eye of hook and conventional knot that attaches the fly to leader is important because it effects how the fly fishes and the kind of wake it produces. It also determines how high up in the water column the fly will ride. A riffled fly will rise surprisingly high in the surface film, and sometimes the angler may not want this.

A fly tied with a ruff or bubblehead need not have a riffle hitch applied in order to make it bob-and-weave in the current. In fact, to tie such a hitch on this kind of a fly is a form of overkill; it is detrimental to correct fly behavior. Like a lot of things, if a little is good, a lot may be worse. I think I prefer a fly tied to riffle, rather than one *made* to do it. A Wulff wing (tied with white calf, which floats about as well as anything in this world, greased or ungreased) will riffle, all by itself. And such a wing—tied slanted forward, either divided or as a solid wing—is easy to see in broken water. Lee Wulff always knew what he was doing. Wulff tied his dries commercially with a single wing at first, but when they didn't sell divided them. Anglers responded to the familiar design element, and bought and fished them avidly.

In broken water—the best kind—a fly can be terribly hard to see. There is a lot of reality to be encountered on a river that is not anticipated in one's easy chair, reading a book like this one. One is wind. A river has a prevailing wind that "springs up" around eleven o'clock, as Hemingway warned us. It strengthens throughout the day, especially on a dropping barometer. Few of the fly-casting books pay much attention to wind, but wind is what will send a novice or intermediate fisher home in a hurry, with a sore arm or a fly in his ear.

If you fish from the right bank (the bank is the one you are on, while facing downstream, towards the river's mouth), an upstream wind is hazardous to a right-handed caster and requires him to make adjustments, such as canting his rod tip into the wind and—alas—hurrying his backcast, which also shortens his effective casting distance. This is frustrating and discouraging.

Broken water, where fish like to be, provides problems that even Polaroid lenses won't eliminate. Many flies have white wings (I don't think fish *like* white wings, by the way) so that the angler can spot his fly in the frothy stuff. So a beginning fisher goes out on the water to catch a steelie, ties on a suitable nondescript fly, heaves it out into the start of the current— and it disappears. He casts again, the fly disappears again. And the next time. It is invisible to him.

There are several things he can do. One is to immediately change to a fly with white on it somewhere—usually in the wing but possibly in a forward hackle. Or he can keep fishing blindly. This is not as bad as it sounds. Steelhead require a slow strike, and the confirmed trout fisher is inclined to hit back way too fast, and either take his fly away from the steelhead or, worse, pop the leader. A slow strike, the kind that takes place from an unheeding angler, often will hook a fish in the best way possible.

Or the fisher can follow the fly by its wake, once the current has begun to slow. This way, he can see it about two-thirds of the time, which is not a bad average. And there is a third thing he can do, one which I try frequently. It is to fish blind intentionally, usually right into the sun, late in afternoon, when you can't see a thing.

I think steelhead (and perhaps trout, too) like a fly fished from this angle. I don't know why, for if the fisher can't see the fish, the fish is better able to see the fisher, and thus should be less receptive to an offering on the surface. The opposite seems true. This is exciting fishing. And I think I enjoy the handicap of temporarily induced sun blindness.

I miss the strike entirely, since I can't see it. But I know something has happened, and react instinctively. I strike slowly, hesitantly, cautiously, doubtfully. Was that a fish . . . or not? In the length of time it takes to pose the question and react to the possible presence of a fish, the late strike arrives at just the right moment. Zip. The fish is hooked in the hinge of the jaw or along the gum line. And then it is off and running, while you look straight into the sun (I hope you are wearing a peaked cap with a green underbill and Polarized glasses) and try to figure out what is happening from the pull on the rod and the scream of the reel. It is the most thrilling time in fly fishing and quickly separates the cool from the uncool, the skilled from the perpetually bumbling.

NINE

O nce upon a time, when there were lots of dour steelhead around and the water was low and warm, I got the notion that the number of wise old fish I could bring up on top was in direct proportion to the lightness of my leader. Year-round, for wet-fly fishing I use eight-pound test of German manufacture; usually for dry fly I try to stay with six. Six works fine, so long as you are careful and don't horse a fish. When the fish is not running—is quiet or coming toward you—six will take a lot more pressure than most people give it credit for.

Four and three are a different matter. I went down to four, then to three. I was getting a fair number of strikes and the fish seemed to be supporting my theory. Since they were wild little Deer Creek steelhead (with a few bigger hatchery ones mixed in, to make matters difficult), what difference did it make if I broke one off—or, as we often put it, "put one back early"? About this time Curt Kraemer showed me his fly box full of surface flies. I liked one very much and went home that night and tied several just like it.

It had a tail of fox squirrel, a golden/orange body, and a divided and forward-tipped wing of fox squirrel again. No hackle. It was designed—like Haig-Brown's Steelhead Bee, and colored much like it—to ride low in the water and to wake. It also resembled Bill Bakke's Dragon Fly. I tied it small—small Wilsons were all I had left, not my ordinary larger hooks, 6s and 8s, which equate to 6s and 4s in somebody else's irons—and thought it would fish best on a light leader. There were sea-run cutthroat in the river, too, and it was a fly—twitched a little on the retrieve—I was certain would attract them, too. This proved correct.

The first night I hooked and landed a seven-pound steelhead headed for Deer Creek on the new fly and the three-pound test leader. It was a good fish and the water I played it in was designed for just such an encounter, with a mild current and lots of slack on my side into which to guide the fish. The only trouble came near the end of the fight when the fish stubbornly refused to be turned and led to the beach. Instead, it kept boring ahead, its back and tail out of the water, wriggling hard; that motion carried the fish upstream and ever toward the sand, where finally unable to remain upright, it toppled over on its side and lay in the shallows, helpless. I unhooked and released it, pretty proud of myself and my light-leader technique.

The next night was nearly a repeat. The fish was about a pound heavier and took in nearly the same place. The fight was about the same—good, but not spectacular. Well, the water was warm, the pool confining, the fish dour. I had a good feel now for what three-pound test leader material would bear and what it wouldn't. The big fear was the fish's teeth raking across it and abrading it. I never thought about my lack of finesse.

Again the fish proved difficult to bring in through the last twenty feet to the beach, but this time it didn't bore upstream and ground itself. It stayed out in the edge of the current and held its position. I moved upstream, I moved downstream. I applied coaxing sidestrain and waited. Nothing happened. The fish maintained its fixed distance from me. Directly opposite now, I tightened a little bit more, for it was necessary to make the fish move. The leader popped and the fish swam away.

I had lost the battle. No matter now that the fish, if landed, would be returned to the river. In the game we play with ourselves, I had miscalculated and the fish had won. It beat me cleanly. Or I had simply beaten myself. Enough with three-pound test leader. Based on this admittedly small sampling, I decided that even with the most careful playing and in quiet water, I would land a well-hooked fish about half the time or less. That was not good enough odds.

I suppose I could have played that fish until the pair of us was exhausted. That is not my way. I gave myself fifteen percent more time than with a heavier leader. I was not about to have a Sam Peckinpaw-type encounter with a fish. I was not going to diddle around with it in the shallows until it was so tired it was unlikely to survive. I wanted a good fish to remain strong and recover quickly. In warm water, a fish doesn't have the recovery rate of a cold-water fish that is newly arrived in the river. It can exhaust itself (or be worn out by the angler) past the point of surviving. I think fifteen minutes is about the most time a fish ought to be battled under these conditions.

You can usually tell when a fish has been played too long by the length of time it takes for it to regain its strength and begin "breathing" again. But this is too late. Often the recovery time becomes excessive, and you feel lucky when the fish swims away with a good beat of its tail, headed for deep water. Deer Creek fish are known to exhaust themselves, running and jumping, time after time, and when the water warms, the chance of death grows great. What is so wonderful about these fish, and makes them worth seeking, is the same quality that threatens their lives when we manage to hook and play them: Their speed and acrobatics jeopardize their survival rate. It is one of those ironical situations that never satisfactorily resolves itself in the fisher's mind and must be addressed anew each year.

The biological answer to the problem is to stop fishing when the water becomes too warm and the number of wild steelhead are so much reduced from their historical run size. But the angler in me says, no, keep fishing for them, but keep a close eye on the river bottom for any signs of mortality—your fish or another's.

It is easy to spot a dead fish in so shrunken a river. Often in late summer the bottom of the pool is lined with dead salmon, humpies and Chinooks—and a steelhead corpse will be easy to identify. My vow is, if I ever see a dead steelhead that can be attributed to me, I will quit until the return of cool weather. This means rain, cold nights, and the greater river flows of fall. It is also the time when all the Deer Creek steelhead will have escaped into the sanctuary waters and there will be no more such fish until spring of the following year.

With a little good luck, I mean.

TEN

Lee Wulff (the father of modern fly angling) makes a good case for the short rod. But in doing so, he makes an even better one for the long. I love fishing with a long rod, winter and summer. Though I have rods of many lengths—six feet up to fourteen and a half—the one I invariably use measures eleven feet, three inches. It is a Sage blank. With it I can dry-fly fish all day. And I can mend and control line quite precisely with little effort.

Wulff's argument, though, has merit; any statement about fishing coming from him automatically does. Lee speaks about the ability to achieve faster line speed with a short rod, with its shorter arc and fulcrum. This, he says, requires a higher degree of athleticism; in other words, you have to be somewhat muscular and well-coordinated, qualities that he had and admired in others. Well, I'm not a jock, but I'd say I possess ordinary strength and coordination. Yet I'm lazy. I like to cast effortlessly, with little need for close timing and great coordination. I like my life and my fishing to proceed easily—easy. Lee correctly points out that the short rod allows less room for error in playing a fish. Because it is so quick to respond to a fish's moves, there is a corresponding need for the angler to compensate quickly, or else the fish will break him off. Lee likes this element, but I do not. He sees the battle with the fish as a one-on-one tussle—which of course it is. He wants to narrow the odds in the fish's favor, which is admirable. But he still wants to win. Make no mistake about it, Lee Wulff always wants to win.

There are other ways to get to the finish line. My fresh-run steelhead are often more than a match for me. A high percentage of my spring fish lick me, straightaway. I want the odds to turn in my favor.

Lee's final argument is his weakest, I think. He speaks of the increased difficulty in presenting the fly to the fish and in making line mends or corrections. Since this is most of what I do, all day long, with no fish responding, I want this "difficult" element made easier. I want gentle mends and graceful presentations, hour after hour, while I'm waiting for what is often the one strike of the day.

I regret that I never got to fish with Lee Wulff; we never got any closer than the mailbox. It would have been a privilege to be outfished (which without a doubt would be the case) by The Master, and the upside of taking such a beating is how much you might learn in the process. Besides, being beaten in a day's fishing by Lee Wulff would be a compliment of the highest order. And, I'm sure this has happened—over the long years of his life—an occasional odd angler was high rod for the day when fishing with Wulff.

Yet I picture Lee on one of his many rivers in New Brunswick or Quebec. Since he is the total fisher, he scarcely notices the strong upstream wind blowing that, from the right bank, makes casting a terror for most of us. He simply accelerates the line speed, tightens the "oval" of his loop, and proceeds to drive the line into the teeth of the wind—not into his forearm, as we would. Here his athleticism prevails. But I suspect it will not be very gainly or graceful to watch, for a steelhead or Atlantic salmon fisher must achieve his daily distance. It is hard work. He cannot be content with the short casts that serve the trout fisher well.

If I were to fish as Lee Wulff did, with the short rod in the wind, I would immediately hook myself in the ear. And since both Wulff and I believe in the efficacy of barbed hooks, there would be trouble ahead. I've only had one hook removed from my anatomy, and it was one driven into my thumb when my hand slipped when tying a leader to a small hook and drawing the knot up tight. It cost me a two-hour trip to the emergency room of the nearest hospital and $80. I would greatly like to prevent a similar occurrence. A long rod, I know, will keep the hook fairly far away from my head, back, and arm. That is another reason I like them.

Guide John Farrar, arguing eloquently and overly long before the Wildlife Commission, once spoke in favor of the universal use of barbless hooks. He said that he has often had to pluck one out of his arm. It is as easy to do, he continued, as releasing a fish. John is a superior caster; he knows what he is talking about. But—like my mentor—I like to use barbed hooks. It takes me only a moment longer to release my fish and I am certain the fish undergoes only a modicum more trauma. I like barbed hooks for the same reason Lee does: they permit me to slacken my line while playing a fish and not lose it when I do.

I slacken my line because it enables me to play the fish much more quickly than if I engaged in a game of tug-o'-war. When the fish runs, I let it run lightly (Hardy reels are wonderful for this, for their checkwork is unwilling to tighten up to the degree necessary to resist a fish's run, only enough to keep the spool from overrunning) until it stops of its own accord; then I return the pressure to the maximum the leader will bear. This is another verse from the Lee Wulff songbook.

A barbless hook, under slack-line conditions, will permit the fish to shake it free, or in some other way eject it. How do I know this? I've had it happen, only with a beaten fish on a short line and a barbed hook. I'd gone two-hundred feet to my car for a camera with which to record the fish's individual beauty. The fish patiently waited in the shallows on a slack line. It could neither escape nor spit out my hook.

It is possible, in fact, to rest a tired fish on a slack line before the final act of releasing it, thereby allowing it to recover from the exhausted state playing it so often involves. I don't know precisely what is involved, biologically speaking. I've heard talk of "lactic acid" build-up in the muscle tissue and I recognize that the swim bladder (which keeps the fish upright, all the while) is often involved, for an exhausted fish is unable to keep itself from going belly up, even in an eddy. Such a fish has to be held in a vertical position and its gills encouraged to work again. Often this takes several minutes, during which time the fish's life is in jeopardy. Guiding a fish into a slough or resting a fish in a back current until release are two ways to let it recover on its own. The fish remains calm, no longer struggling, and the barbed hook can be quickly reversed in its hold with a pair of needle-nosed pliers.

I go into all this because the length of the rod, the speed of the line, the need for frequent line corrections early and mid-way through the drift, and the care in playing a fish are all important elements in the course of a successful or unsuccessful day. I much prefer to have a good one, as people keep urging me to do in grocery stores. A long rod, but one that is untiring to cast, is what I choose to fish with, most any day. And a barbed hook—where the regulations permit its use—is the perfect accompaniment, for it contributes to the fish's capture and chance of survival. In this day of reduced wild-fish runs, a steelhead's recovery is more important than at any time in the past.

ELEVEN

Anybody who has fished very much for steelhead or salmon has seen a picture of A.H.E. Wood, of Cairnton, Scotland, and the River Dee, standing atop a jetty and casting one-handedly a huge bamboo rod intended for ordinary mortals to exercise with both hands. (In pictures it looks like a rock he is standing on, but he had a bum leg and could not wade; thus, he had jetties built on his beat, which of course he owned.) Back before fiberglass and long before graphite, many of us tried to repeat Wood's feat with cane and were delivered early to the showers.

It is no longer necessary to punish yourself as he did.

Two-handed rods are in vogue. Oh, are they. Every steelheader worth his salt now owns one or two. They are not made of bamboo or greenheart or even fiberglass, as in the past; they are made of relatively light-weight graphite and, chances are, were designed by Jimmy Green, formerly of Fenwick and Sage.

I have an early two-handed graphite rod and clumsily made it cast long and catch fish for me on the Sauk. I did (and do) not know the range of Spey casts, and simply "threw it out there." I fished such a rod before Trey Combs had tried one; it was, in fact, how I met him. He was curious about mine and its applications for steelhead. Soon he was taking lessons from

A.H.E. Wood

Mike Maxwell of Vancouver, B.C. and mastering single and double Spey casts from both banks. He is skilled at them. He has written about Spey rods extensively in his omnibus *Steelhead Fly Fishing*. No doubt about it, such rods cast a fly an enormous distance and, when you do it correctly, with little effort. But how often do you need to do this? Surely not in the summer on most streams. And for dry-fly fishing they lack subtlety and slam the fly down hard, many times. I have put mine aside except for extreme winter or spring conditions. More and more I find the long one-handed rod does most of my work.

One spring I used a loaner Spey rod. It was made by Gary Loomis and never, I believe, put into production. It was sixteen-feet long and there quickly developed a problem with tiny cracks appearing in the self-ferrule. These cracks did not ruin the rod, which proved structurally strong, but they made me distrustful. I could picture the rod snapping during one of the vigorous line pickups or during the violent forward cast that follows, and I would be responsible for the damage. But the main reason I stopped using it was different.

It was spring, and I had long walks ahead along a river trail to reach the next pool that I hoped would be productive. Salmonberry was blooming and blackberry was creeping across the trail, and whoever laid out that trail did not have a sixteen-foot rod in mind to tow through the brush. The rod kept catching on boughs behind me—naturally I proceeded down the trail with the rod butt in front of me, so as not to snag the tip and snap it off before I could grind my feet to a stop. So the rod trailed behind me, catching its guides or tiptop or strung line on the branches to the rear or, worse, getting trapped between tree trunks as the trail made a steep turn and the rod did not.

Gary's rods all have a beautiful finish. This one's was burgundy, with a high gloss. I virtually destroyed the finish by carrying it through the newly emerging greenery of a Stillaguamish spring. When the gloss was nicked, the undercoat of the rod showed a different color—brown. I bought a felt-tipped marker close enough to match, and after a day's wanderings touched up the rod so that it looked less scratched and worn. Finally, when the ferrule problem became pronounced, I returned the rod to its rightful owner, Nick Gayeski, and got my half of the tariff back. Soon I stopped carrying my own $135 Lamiglas double-handed rod out to the river, too; I didn't like that much baggage.

There is something highly enjoyable about going out in the woods traveling light. Of course, like everybody else, I load up my fishing vest with fly boxes, extra reels or spools, rain jacket, collapsible wading staff, etc., until it reaches its requisite fifteen pounds or so. But I like everything else to be minimal and easy. The rod— here Arthur Wood keeps coming to mind—must be long enough to do the work required of it, but light enough to be a pleasure to hold and cast and mend with, throughout a long day.

Most anglers don't like to go over nine feet with a rod intended for dry-fly use. Frank Amato is one of these. Like many accomplished anglers, he has many rods, but most of them are nine feet long. Some are capable of casting lines so light as twos, threes, and fours. I know what he is after. He likes easy, effortless fishing, with a line just as gossamer as possible to reach the longest distance he is apt to want to cover on a given river on a certain day. And for a reel, he has codified his selection to the Orvis CFO, which is well-ventilated and light in weight. It comes, or rather used to come, in a great range of sizes. The model V—the only one really right for steelhead, in my opinion—was discontinued a few years ago. Most models are suitable for trout. With fine backing and a dry line cut back from its rear end, however, they can be pressed to serve (as will the Hardy light-weight series) for steelhead. This is another case of handicapping oneself to the fish's advantage, as Lee Wulff did, and I can appreciate it.

I hate to lug around a rod so long and heavy as a Spey. To balance it in the act of casting, it needs a heavy reel. I don't know what one of them weighs, but it is considerable. I do know what a one-handed rod and reel weigh, and it isn't much. True, my long one-handed rod is subject to some of the same drawbacks of walking along a trail as the long Spey rods, but it never seems so bad. Maybe the difference in length of a few feet is critical. I do know that short rods are easy to carry and weigh even less. They were originally designed for small trout on brushy streams. Leave it to a Lee Wulff to use them for giant fish.

Midge rods are better, though, for dry-fly steelhead on small summer rivers than Spey rods are. And much more fun. It is a challenge which I have written about before to catch steelhead on a rod that is by definition under two ounces in finished weight. It is a further challenge to catch two wild steelhead (a limit) on such a rod and a tiny reel with thread-like backing and to release them, all in a day. But to set out on a windy summer stream to fish all day long a wide reach of water with only a midge rod is a nightmare. Each year I am less likely to do it.

TWELVE

It is impossible, after so much time has passed, and so many technical innovations have taken place, to step into the mind of A.H.E. Wood and grasp what he was after when he practiced the "greased-line" technique of fishing he made famous. (See Jock Scott, *Greased Line Fishing for Salmon [and Steelhead]*, Frank Amato Publications, Inc., 1982.) It was a method he stumbled on in Ireland, according to Alec Jackson, the authority.

Yet try we must. For instance, he did not think of ways to make his fishing more difficult. When you look at the enormous bags of big salmon he regularly took, his goal was simply to kill fish, or more fish. Subtlety be hung. He stood on his jetty and swung his giant rod as an athlete would do (or as Lee Wulff might have done, in that day, at least until shorter rods were manufactured to his specs), and cast his line in such a manner that his fly would come across the nose plane of resident salmon in a way that it might pass straight through their mouths, left to right or, as the case might be, right to left. If he did it correctly—right fly pattern, right fly size, right fly speed— the salmon would glom onto the fly and be hooked in the opposite hinge of the jaw. Then Arthur Wood would be happy.

It happened often.

Wood did not fish a floating line because it was sporting. He did it because it was all he had. Silk—left ungreased—would sink naturally in spring's high flow, especially if a big, heavy fly were attached. (They don't call 'em "irons" for nothing.) Silk, greased to float to keep it out of the rocks on the bottom during low flows, would allow his fly to ride just under the surface but not lodge in the rocks and become lost. It is the same situation we steelheaders face from August on in our favorite West Coast rivers and on the rivers to the East, which are greatly reduced for irrigation purposes, becoming ghosts of their springtime selves. We want to keep off the bottom, if for no other reason than to keep from losing so many flies. But we want to stay high up in the water column because we know the fish are now oriented to that level and we will be fishing most effectively for them there.

All the diagrams in Jock Scott's book about Wood's greased-line mending only confuse the issue. Those myriad actions are simply what an experienced angler does to make his fly behave naturally in various conflicting currents—some of them tiny and all much smaller than earlier in the year. Wood's rivers formed back eddies, too, when they attained their annual drop. A back eddy at the edge of a pool with normally a strong, straightforward flow is more than a nuisance. It is a hazard. The line bags and comes drifting back at you and the fly sags on its leader and the bend of the hook swings downward, becoming one of those initial question marks with which the Spanish begin an interrogatory sentence. If a fish takes a fly presented thus it is an anomaly. You deserve no credit for it and chances are it will not happen again for a long while.

Mending—in spite of the dedication with which some anglers perform it, hour after hour—is not virtuous. It has no value in itself. It is not a requirement but a means to an end, that end being to make the fly behave as though alive and not some inert piece of metal with feathers attached. Each mend ought to have a purpose. The main function is to defeat the belly in the line, which drags the fly around in a speedy, unnatural manner—unless the water is truly slack, in which case, the belly may be capitalized upon and even abetted by adding to it to give the fly the touch of speed it would otherwise be lacking. The idea is not to eliminate drag, which is impossible, but to control it. Wood defined drag as when you could feel the line pulling on the rod. In very slack water you might want more. Adding to the drag is called "pulling through" by the British, and it will occasionally result in taking a fish that would otherwise turn its nose up at your offering.

Arthur Wood mended because he had to. He didn't want to lift that telephone pole of a rod any higher or any more often than he had to, and he had to each time he made a cast—raising, loading, and flinging the commensurately heavy line the shortest necessary distance in order to fish the water in which he knew one or more salmon lay.

I can picture him, as often I envision him from his fuzzy photos; he doesn't look so different from me, but is stronger, smarter, taller, etc. He is no less lazy than he has to be. Lift, load, fling. "Throw it out there," as Lee Wulff says about casting. That's all there is to it. Mend, if you have to. With a long rod, there is such a thing as "lifting over." It can be characterized as a half-mend. The longer the rod, the easier it is to accomplish and the less effort it takes. I suppose Lee Wulff could do it with a tiny rod, but I know it isn't easy. Well, Lee Wulff didn't like things easy.

Wood fished every day except Sunday. Sundays, he cleaned his big Hardy reels. It was important for him to keep his reels (they are basically the same reels as mine, only mine are lighter weight and a tad smaller) clean and freely running because some of his fish were huge and would cause a spring or pawl or even the housing to shatter if they were not kept free of grit and lightly oiled. Me, I'm careless, as well as lazy, and don't clean and oil mine as frequently as I should. Occasionally I break a pawl or spring because it is dry and subject to too much sudden strain. Usually it is not from a fish but merely from hurriedly stripping off line to make my first cast in a fresh pool. Ping and I'm into free-spool.

A few times, though, a fish has been on the end of the line and the results are, well, interesting. I think everybody should have the opportunity to play a fine fish on a reel with absolutely no click, drag, or resistance. It is a life experience, as they say about some other awful matters. I would never willingly choose to put myself in such a situation, but I have found myself there and have not lost the fish, let me add. Immediately I repaired and oiled the reel, for I was not anxious to repeat the event. (Hardys carry an internal set of spares for just this reason. But only one set.)

Wood avoided this problem by systematically cleaning his reels once a week. It is the ideal length of time, Sunday to Sunday. On Monday you can start out knowing there is no fish in the river capable of taking you apart and putting you back together in less than the desirable order.

THIRTEEN

Mending. Let us talk further about this fascinating subject. It has to do with avoiding belly, except in those few cases where belly or even more belly is desired.

What is wrong with belly? Well, it shows the fish the line before it sees the fly. That's one thing and a big one. And it affects fly speed, almost always for the worse, hauling the fly around in the current faster than it would ordinarily proceed, if it were a tiny bait fish or an insect. Of course the fish has probably not seen a fly before, so the matter is theoretical.

Point of fact: a fly behaves in the current rather peculiarly, do what you may to make it act otherwise. The problem is belly again, and mending is only part of the corrective action. The belly of the line is what gives it weight, which is what enables us to cast it. The belly is thicker and heavier than the rest of the line. The line has a tip, which graduates from the belly and reduces itself again into the leader, which is tapered. It is either tapered invisibly or with knots. At the end of the finest section is tied a fly.

At the other end of the belly—and this distance varies considerably, depending on whose floating line it is—is some thinner substance called running line. True, a double-taper line has no running line, and this is why some anglers prefer it, though it cannot be cast so far as a forward-taper line. (On a Spey rod a double-taper is preferred, at least in Scotland, where it originated, and is the only type of line that will cast a great distance, but never mind; it is not what we are concerned with here.) A double-tapered line can be mended beautifully, and it can be roll cast. The FFF now has a qualifying test for fly casting instructors and one of the early challenges is to be able to roll cast fifty-five feet. I don't think I can do it, not with most of my rods and lines, but then I have no occasion. I can do a kind of flip and pick up at about that distance. It is all I need to do to be able to fish easily, load up my long one-handed rod, and shoot a line, oh, say, seventy feet, with a single backcast. I'd like to see the FFF-qualified instructors do that!

But this is about mending and how one shouldn't mend any more than is necessary to achieve one's goal, which is making the fly behave in such a lifelike manner as to have a salmon or steelhead intercept it. (Don't ask me why they do this, I have no answer. Each year I marvel at the fact that they will, whatever their weird reasons. Probably it is because they are just as bored as I am. After all, spawning for both of us is pretty far off.)

A mend is a roll or liftover of line with the goal of accomplishing some intended purpose having to do with reducing the pull of the belly unnaturally in the current and keeping it from making the fly do something you believe it shouldn't be doing at this particular moment. You should always have a good reason to mend and not do it routinely.

The mend is best performed without moving the fly, only the line and leader butt. There are exceptions. Occasionally you may wish to jerk the fly around in the water and position it vastly different from before. This should not happen often. Better it is to fish out the cast and do it differently, more carefully, next time. After all, it is a long day, and there are many casts left in it. You need only one or two performed excellently to catch a fish, it only holds to reason. Of course fish do not respond to reason. It is why we love 'em.

Mends for the dry fly always turn out differently from what I intend. The flip that I want to correct the dry fly's drift often drags it under. Later on in the drift, the great looping mend I make in order for the fly to fish effectively another four or five feet, and which I expect to drown it, merely half-corrects the fly's course and doesn't even make it dip. And often I will strip in line like crazy, thinking I have gone too far—and the fly will still be floating merrily along on its downstream course, undisturbed, unaffected. If I had struck a fish just as hard, I wouldn't have moved the fly enough to set the hook. But I don't know this for a fact until I've done it (or not done it), and looked aghast at the futility of my effort.

For once it wasn't extreme enough.

FOURTEEN

In the movie, *A River Runs Through It,* which every fisherman worth his neoprenes must have seen in the theater, rather than wait for it to come to home video, there is a scene where Tom Skerritt instructs his sons on how to flycast the old-fashioned way. The father is a staunch Presbyterian minister, with a classic metronomic style. The rod is not to go back past the vertical on the backcast. Likewise, the elbow of the casting arm is to be kept clamped to the ribcage; a book under the arm will be supplied, if the rule is ever violated. (The book may even be the Good Book. Don't let it fall to the

Tom Skerritt

ground! Your life depends!)

Back and forth through the air goes the rod, closely followed by the line. The rod is bamboo, probably eight and one-half or nine feet in length, most likely the latter. The laws of physics can be drawn upon to determine just how far a double-tapered line can be cast with this gear and this method. My guess is about fifty-five feet.

That is plenty far enough to catch a mess of trout from a Montana stream, fifty years ago. Or even today.

It is not far enough to catch a steelhead, most of the year—today or yesteryear. That is about the minimum distance for a cast.

This year the distance across the bottom of the Manure Spreader Hole, where the river fans out and there are bank pockets, is about one-hundred and ten feet. I can't cast that far.

How far can I cast a rocket-taper dry line, standing on the beach, with a medium strong wind coming to my disadvantage, as it always seems to be doing? Ankle-deep in the river—which is in far enough. With some stones starting about forty feet behind me. I'm not sure, but let us say I am consistently falling twenty feet short of hitting the bank. Probably much more. Yes, I know: Go get your Spey rod. Well, I won't.

The trout fishers that come to my river in search of sea-run cutthroats satisfy themselves with fishing the slack on the near side. Ninety percent of the cutts and most of the steelhead are on the far side. It is where I would be found, this sunny day, with the only available shade for half a mile in either direction.

Even if I could hit the bank, I would be unable to sink a wet fly to the fish's depth before the current whips it to the center of the river and it begins to sink nicely. And with a dry fly and line, there is a back eddy so far over in which the fly will hang, hang, until the current grabs the belly and whips the fly in a speedy arc to the center of the river, where it begins to bob-and-weave the way I wanted it to earlier. But I can put it in that location without so long a cast—and without all the hanging and whipping that follows. So I am virtually unable to fish the holding slots along the riprap on the far side, for a variety of reasons. The fish are safe, for now and all time.

If the North Fork were open in the summer to the use of spinning tackle, or bait, an accomplished angler could effectively cover these difficult locations and, one by one, the cutthroats and steelhead would succumb. I know they would, for I've done it elsewhere. It was long ago, and I don't want to talk about it. I was a boy and the stream a different one. Besides, all of us dedicated fly fishers have a poacher's heart, not buried very deep. We know what it takes, in a given situation, to get that fish on the beach.

It's just that we've vowed not to do it anymore.

FIFTEEN

So how do we cast, if not like Tom Skerritt and his movie sons? Why, full arm and as unlike a metronome as possible. And we do not lengthen out our long lines through repeated false casting. False casting is false. We want the line to go out there as quickly as possible. Our casts drift back, back, over our shoulder, until the rod is in a near-horizontal plane. What, won't the fly strike the rocks?

No, not if it is moving rapidly enough. The idea is to keep it up in the air, with the line speed so fast it hasn't time to drop. The longer the fulcrum arm, the farther the line and fly will go. This again is ordinary physics.

There are three ways to lengthen the fulcrum arm. One is to increase the length of the rod. (My favorite.) The second is to widen the arc until it comes close to 180 degrees; this is about twice what the minister told his boys. They didn't question the ninety-degree principle. It was Gospel. The third way is to increase the line speed. To do this, a short rod has to be moved rapidly; Wulffian athleticism is called for. But if the rod is longer, the line speed can be increased without so much effort. Applied physics again.

The only possible drawback to increased line speed with a long rod is if the rod is heavy. It'll wear you out in no time. Graphite rods have pretty much eliminated the problem. But a Spey rod is both long and heavy. It can't be moved very fast, even by the athletic. Instead, it makes use of other principles to deliver long casts. To understand these one has to behold the lyric beauty of a well-executed Spey cast and watch the line sailing out its fantastical distance.

But this is not for me or the situations I am describing. Another time, perhaps.

The rod picks up the line, quickly, powerfully, telling it where it is to go—that is back and away. The rod drifts with the line, reaches the historical vertical limit and transcends it, going, back, back, until it is in the horizontal plane. The rod then "catches" the line and reverses its direction. None of the above can be executed in a tentative manner. The line has to be firmly instructed in what to do and where to go.

The line's job is to load the rod. A rod is best loaded as much as it will tolerate. Since graphite is so strong, there is little danger in breaking the rod while casting it. There is a greater chance of you hurting your arm or shoulder. (We should have a separate chapter on caster's injuries and how to prevent them. They are much easier to avoid than to get healed, once they have taken place.) Lee Wulff has likened the right casting action to trying to throw an apple off the end of a stick. Nowhere has he explained how the apple got there in the first place. I guess he stuck it on in order to shake it off with a precise motion that is like the forward cast. Me, I started out with an apple and a stick, ate the apple, and threw away the stick. But, yes, the motion is a little like that. Yet it is different.

Wulff (and his wife, Joan, an accomplished caster and instructor) have also likened this motion to prescribing an oval with the rod and line. It is a good analogy; whenever a Wulff speaks, it behooves us to pay close attention, and we are never the worse for it. The motion of a line being picked up off the water, directed back over your shoulder—up and away—is indeed much like drawing an oval in the air with your rod and its tip. It is also like making a circle. The oval or circle is slightly tipped outward, that is, the bottom of it is closer to your hip and the top of it is pointed away from your shoulder. The harder the wind is blowing the more the oval or circle approaches the horizontal plane and the farther away from your head the top of the circle will be.

Picture this, then. You are drawing a circle in the air with a stick that has an apple on the end of it. At the end of its Ferris-wheel ride you are prescribing, you try to fling the occupants of the top car (or the apple on the stick) as far as you can in the direction of a fence that marks the boundary of the fairgrounds. Or in the case of the apple and stick, toward an imaginary basket in which you intend the apple to land like a basketball, some eighty feet away. Or on top of a fish's ring, where it has just risen, about the same distance away.

Clear? That's all we need to know about casting, or do Tom Skerritt's sons.

SIXTEEN

I firmly believe that a pool may house steelhead or salmon throughout its length, and some of those fish will respond to a floating line and surface or riffling fly, while others will be interested only in a fly that is drifting slowly along near the bottom. What is more, I believe that the one fish can become the other fish during the course of a lazy afternoon. It all depends

Tom Crawford

on where the fish is lying and its inclination. Ah, that inclination. Is it important? It is all.

Merlin's Pool on the Wenatchee is a good example. One night I fished it wet. G. L. Britten who owns a fly-fishing store in Spokane followed me through it dry and, halfway down, hooked a fine fish. I clambered out of the water so he would have room to play it, which he did deftly and soon landed and released it. Then it was dark.

Another night I fished the pool dry and took a fine fish, the man ahead of me and the one behind me hooking nothing, wet. But I have followed a dry man through the pool fishing wet and taken one fish, two fish, three. Once Tom Crawford came in behind me, when I was fishing wet. He went through the water I had just seined and took a fine, small fish dry. Another time in the same pool, at the same low height, Tom was fishing a ten-foot sink-tip line in extreme low water; I came in behind him and *in one cast* (you remember these things, especially when fishing behind a skilled fisher like

Tom) with a twenty-foot tip took a fish. Of course I pointed out to Tom that one cast was all some people needed to catch a steelhead.

In this same pool, having it all to myself, I've fished it wet, then followed myself through it, dry, and taken a fish, as though I were another person. (This is a way of fishing I enjoy very much. It calls for a split personality.) There is something simply wonderful about hooking a big fish in such water, which tends to be stillish, on a fly you can barely see and keep losing sight of in broken water. Often the fish will hit or bunt it and return on the very next cast to take it solidly. The take is soft, but the softness is gone the instant you tighten. And some of these fish go up to sixteen pounds and are by definition wild, retaining their adipose fins, while of course being descended from hatchery stock.

Last year, fishing dry and lightly riffled, one night I took a strange fish of about sixteen inches. It looked to be a rainbow, but was very dark. Taking a closer look before releasing it, I saw it was a jack Chinook. It had a long anal fin and black gums. Otherwise, it was spotted much like a spawning rainbow. Of course they don't spawn at this time of year, which was fall. The fish was a good fighter and I was happy to hook and play it, for there was no steelhead for me that night. The next evening, I took two such fish, both on the surface. They were nearly identical. One might be a fluke, two a coincidence, but three was surely a trend. What were such fish doing in the river, let alone attacking surface flies that greatly resembled natural food? I pondered the matter, but could come up with no satisfactory answer.

I thought the fish might be from hatchery plants that had gone to sea and come back with the adults of the previous class. But wouldn't they be a lot bigger? I should think so. And all of those dams to descend and ascend. Why? To spawn with bigger fish for some obscure biological reason that had to do with the reason for jacks in the first place—to ensure continuity of the race of fish in the event of one or more natural disasters?

I had to wait for the answer. Bill McMillan, writing in the newsletter of Washington Trout about the loss of various salmon and steelhead races in the Columbia system, addressed the matter of hatchery plants of Chinook salmon and said that many of these fish "residualized," meaning they became resident and did not migrate. Of course.

My fish were hatchery Chinook smolts that had decided the dams were too much for them, both coming and going, and they would become like trout and live off the river bounty. It is generally known among fish biologists that Chinook juveniles vary greatly in how old they are before the migrating urge moves them, some leaving the river as early fry, some as one-year-olds that hang around the estuary, feeding for another year before heading out to sea with another year's class. And of those Chinooks in rivers on the West Slope, there are always jacks that return with the adults, fish that look like mine but have estuary or minimal sea feeding.

Such fish are despised by biologists in charge of hatcheries—for one thing, they have no commercial value and represent a management failure, rather than an accomplishment—yet put enough of them in a river and let them forage for food along with the resident trout and juvenile steelhead and you have another species of sport fish, especially if they take surface flies so readily.

I wondered whether it was legal to kill and eat them? It would probably be good to remove them from the river, since they aren't needed to spawn and in fact might be harmful to salmon reproduction, for they would bring down the average size of the race over time. How would they taste? Eating the same food as river trout, they would probably be delicious. Like all small Chinook, they would have white meat, but that is only a visual drawback and might affect how they taste but solely from a psychological viewpoint.

It is illegal to take salmon from this river, at least in the fall, so I would never know about their taste or the color of their flesh. White, certainly. Not much Keratin in river food.

SEVENTEEN

I have been talking about fish in a given pool having different orientations, some inclined towards the surface, while others are still keyed to the bottom, and how the same fish may vary their orientation over the course of a given day simply by changing their lies. And a fish effortlessly moves about a pool at will—with little expenditure of energy and no difficulty—many times daily, so it only holds to reason that the same fish will change its attitude often and repeatedly. So it is worthwhile to fish a favorite pool both wet and dry. Or two good friends can fish it each way at the same time, one following the other, or alternating halves of the pool.

If they do, my opinion is they will be fishing for different fish, even if they do not know it. And they will be systematically covering the water to maximum effectiveness. I do not want to follow another angler through the pool, fishing it the same way as he does—wet or dry—but I see other anglers happily doing it almost daily. It sometimes produces, yes, but it is boring and makes my mind wander. Also, I don't fish well this way. If I must follow somebody, I will fish in the opposite manner usually. It is more interesting and my effectiveness at getting a fish to take increases substantially. Or so I believe.

Besides, we are all searching for the best way to capture a fish that is rightly ours. "Rightly?" If you catch the fish, it is simply a matter of superior skill. And if he catches it? Luck, pure luck.

I never get over my sense of astonishment that big fish will take a surface fly. It looks so unnatural and often there are smaller real insects, caddis or mayflies, bobbing handsomely alongside our offerings that get ignored. Why are ours *ever* taken? Is it because they look so unnatural? Do they provoke the fish, through their strange behavior? Is this why I riffle my fly like crazy, whenever water conditions permit it to behave that way?

Two pools come to mind that fish nicely this way. One is Merlin's Pool on the Wenatchee, the other being the one down from the black rock on the Grande Ronde. Both are long, classic pools formed in bedrock streams that have varied little from year to year. But the great flood of 1990 has changed Merlin's Pool and Jimmy Hunnicut, who knows it well, claims it doesn't hold fish the way it used to. Perhaps, but fishers are always grousing about how much better things were, decades ago. It still holds some fish. It may be that seasons seem better, once some time accumulates between events and the memory of them.

What Jimmy is saying is that, sure, the pool continues to produce fish, but not so many of them as in the past, and I agree. But let a pool regularly hold some fish and I am happy with it. Merlin's Pool does. The top of the run, however, has filled in with small stones—not peagravel, for the Wenatchee seems to be lacking in this, making up for it now with sand; these stones run from fist-sized up to the size of volleyballs. There are so many of them that the top of the run is much shallower than it used to be and does not provide cover to the same extent. So shallow now, its few fish are easily spooked by the wading fisher and drift back to deeper water. It happens as soon as we enter the river from the beach, I suspect, and we never see them vacating the upper end of the pool.

Merlin's Pool has a wonderful configuration, though, beginning where the river spills over from a big upstream flat and runs against the far bank, leaving a great gravel shoal lunging out into the river and the river narrowing and spilling into a narrow gut against the riprap and widening gradually and slowing until it becomes one of those deep, dead, slab-rock holes which steelheaders from different rivers are used to walking by without making a single cast. On the Wenatchee this is a mistake. It is just such dead water that steelhead love to take up lies in, I don't know why. If I was a steelhead, I surely wouldn't. And a fly fishes through it so slowly, so unexcitingly, that those of us who love fast-water takes are instantly bored and do not contemplate fishing it. This, of course, is repeating the same old mistake.

At the top there were many good, shallow, rocky lies, and the fish sought them. A sink tip line, or else a fly on a floater worked through here, often produced a strike, then another. I have no idea how many fish chose to lie here but it was many. If there were any fish in the river, you could bet your favorite rod a few would rest here and, if not disturbed, would be ready takers.

There are fewer of them now because it is less desirable holding water. And any kind of sinking line will immediately hang up and cause a commotion on the bottom, often with a lost fly and tippet as a result. Fish hang around here, but are apt to be a bit skittish because of the lack of depth and suitable shade. All day long the hot sun bears down on the Wenatchee. The fish get used to it. If you wait for a cloudy day—the steelheader's fervent dream—you will do little fishing.

The top of the pool was designed for the floating fly. Its angle is just right, requiring a few quick mends at the start and, as you move on down through it, not so many mends, for the current straightens out, the pool deepens by degrees, great slabs of sunken sandstone appear, the current slows, and the river widens out to the point that the longest cast falls far short of the distant bank.

The fish lie anywhere and everywhere. After repeated seasons and much fishing, a few locations are found to produce consistently, low water or mid or (if you can reach them then) high. As you fish through the pool, your pulse quickens when you come to one of these proven lies and—if you are anything like me—you become tense with expectation. Often a fish takes just as you expected it to, but often a moment earlier in the drift or with a wallop at the end of it, when you no longer expect one.

I used to maintain I could fish this pool happily once a day for the rest of my life. Of course I mean in season. Rivers with anadromous fish are barren of steelhead and salmon much of the year. And on the Wenatchee, before the start of the annual irrigation withdrawal, the river runs bank-high with snowmelt from the Cascade Mountains. It is practically impossible to fish then, at least with the fly. This is just as well, for there are no fresh fish in the river yet; it is the same time as the previous year's class of fish is spawning, and I suppose a diehard could go out after them, but we don't. It is simply too high to fish anymore than a few shallow flats. These are probably where the fish are on the redds, too and should be protected from molestation.

A floating line with a leader at least nine feet long, tapering down to a tippet of six or eight pounds, is ideal for later. Depending on the weight of the hook it's tied on, a fly can be made to fish on top or down a few inches. It can even be induced to fish near the bottom. So by simply changing flies the fisher can cover the same run in a number of different ways, showing the steelhead a variety of presentations. A fly can be fished dead-drift, up and across, or downstream, with the line being played out of one's hand or from a stripping basket. (Trout too love a fly presented this way, especially in broken water.)

The fly can be skated. It can be waked gently. It can be riffled like my F-7 Flatfish. It can be drifted along in the surface film, half-submerged, like a drowned insect. It can be fished just under the surface, wet, with the line mended as often as necessary to keep the fly's plane at right-angles to the fish, as prescribed in Jock Scott's book on A.H.E. Wood, so that the fly seemingly passes sideways through the fish's jaws (though I've always doubt- ed that this is what truly happens, hooks behaving the way they do). Or it can be fished heedlessly wet-fly style, the line kept taut and the only mends those necessary to prevent the belly from dragging through the pool first.

All these things can be accomplished from the same station that the fish- er has waded to in the current, out only as far as necessary in the run to achieve the right angle of presentation and the correct drift or swing of his fly. How easy it is, how much more casual than sunk wet fly, which requires constant line adjustments to keep the fly deep but off the bottom. And the great advantage is, you can see your line and usually your fly. When the take comes, it is often visible and dramatic.

The shallower the water, the more likely the fish will make a surface rise and immediately go into the air. Its run will be swifter and farther, most like- ly, because a fish panics in such water. In Merlin's Pool, on a surface take, I've had steelhead leap high in the air over my head, only a few yards away. I've had them snatch the fly in a rush and continue on upstream, their backs out of the water, throwing a sharklike wake. I've had them whisk along, a few feet away on the far side of me, and immediately change course and come barrelling down my side, thereby lassoing me with my own line and requiring a quick special mend to free myself.

I've had a big, wild fish come up past me into the top of the riffle, turn, proceed downstream at a speed that gradually slows, and immediately come to a stop in dead water over a hundred yards downstream—all without a pause. So it is only natural I become excited each time I enter this pool and begin my systematic progress through it. Each time I expect something new from the fish and I frequently get it.

Scenic points of interest in Merlin's Pool: (1) the big triangular rock in the water at the top, where Bob Aid historically starts to fish, but which I now find is about fifteen inches deep and marks the place where one can cross—if there is any useful reason to do so, (2) the first square rock out from the bank that looks to be old cement pavement, where the river begins to deepen and the tops of similar chunks start to appear, interspersed with boulders, (3) the lone pine, where many of us believe the pool proper begins now, and where the river begins to widen and deepen and makes casting (especially in the wind) difficult, (4) the culvert, where the unused water from the irrigation diversion is returned to the river; at the season's start there is no water flowing from the pipe, for it is all being used for the apple crop; later, as various fruits are harvested, increasing quantities of water are returned to the river and soon the culvert is roaring, (5) the slow, still, deep water down from the culvert, where the river would be boring, except for the fact that many fine steelhead lie in among the deeply sunken boulders and slab rock, and regularly take here, I don't know why. I'm not a steelhead and my reasoning is different from theirs. (If it wasn't, I would probably catch more fish.)

I can come up with satisfactory reasons why steelhead lie in the upper-middle portion. It is where I (a steelhead again, for the moment) would lie. It has all the requisite characteristics. It is deep, it is fairly fast, it has an uneven mixture of rock sizes and types, among which I can move easily whenever the notion strikes me. Why is it then so many of us are hooked in the dull water below— and in similar places throughout the Wenatchee's full length? I don't know (I am a fly fisher again, please note), but even this bit of information is a big help.

I picture imaginary steelhead lying at the bottom of Merlin's Pool and my fly drifting along, doing stupid things, such as turning hook-point up or riding along upside down. All the flytying materials I lovingly assembled on my flytying bench and put together in the correct proportions for whatever style fly I wanted avail me not: The fly is an awkward piece of metal that has lost its hydrodynamic characteristics in slow water and the materials have become inert; they jut out at weird angles, unnatural and ugly. But steelhead take it. Why?

Steelhead (and I) like a sleek fly that darts through the current, swimmingly. There is no earthly reason why they should take a lifeless fly in this situation. The surface film barely supports the fly, or else fails to support it. If the fly is truly dry, that is, still floating, it lies out there in the currentless river as though trapped on a lake, and any sensible trout or steelhead will see its manifold phoniness—the black steel hook, the foolish hackle, the dumb wing, the cumbersome body. Yet steelhead will rise up out of their depths and nail it. Sometimes they clobber it. Meanwhile, real insects float by, fluttering enticingly, invitingly. These are ignored by all except the passing parr.

I dwell on this aspect because a normal trout or steelhead fisher will reel in early and go on to the next pool. Only a beginner (or one who has learned a lot) will bother with such dull water. After a handful of fish from it, you will begin to approach it keenly. You are ready for the quick take—either a snatch-and-run or else a simple stoppage of your fly, as the fish sucks it in and returns to its earlier station, the fly in its mouth. So often these fish are hooked securely in the hinge of the jaw. It is as though they lie in wait for an unreal fly to come along and then take it as though it were their favorite food, instead of one of the naturals that drift along by the hour, exactly as when they were juveniles.

I simply can't understand it. Which doesn't mean I don't try to capitalize on it or don't look forward to it happening. In fact, I've come to expect it. "Come on fish," I tell them. "Take my fly . . . *now*." And sometimes they do.

They will strike a sunken fly in such water, too. This is more understandable. It comes sliding by them and they either have to get out of its way or mouth it. Often they strike out of annoyance, I am sure. They dislike having their territory invaded by a small, obnoxious-looking creature such as an artificial fly.

The take of a sunk fly on a floating line is usually much like that of a sunk fly on a sunk line. The fish simply stops it. The line continues on its course, bellying out, and the action of the growing weight draws the hook back in the fish's mouth. The increasing pressure of the line on the fish is what goads it into action. The movement is slow at first, for the pressure is slight. Add to the pressure a little by pulling on the line and the fish comes alive. Often it starts its run slowly, unalarmed, and does not panic until the restraint mounts. This is especially true with big fish. The Wenatchee now has fish in the 12-18 pound range, generally males, with adipose fins and tall dorsals that indicate they have no recent hatchery history. These are the progeny of upper Columbia stock, fish planted annually over a decade or more or ones that have spawned successfully in the river.

Big, wonderful fish, they will take a fly on the surface, as well as one fished deep

EIGHTEEN

G rande Ronde fish are not so big, not unless you get a B-race stray from the Clearwater, thirty miles downstream. If you ask me what business a Clearwater giant has going so far past the mouth of its natal river, to which it only has to return, I have no answer for you.

My second classic pool for the floating line is the one which is headed by a big, black rock on the far bank. It is basalt. This is the famous pool up from the mouth on the Ronde that—it is said—receives no sunlight during the course of an October day. It does, I've learned, but only a little, late in the afternoon. It is a fine pool, long enough to accommodate six or eight anglers (if you should be so unlucky) and holds fish throughout its length. When the thermal block goes out and fish from the Snake decide it is time to ascend because of the lure of colder water, they run up from the mouth in large numbers. The pool with the black rock is often where they stop to rest for an hour or so, as it is the first slow water up from the mouth. Moving steelhead will lie briefly almost anywhere in this run, which is two-hundred yards long or more.

And when there are no fish reported in the river, it is a good place to find the odd one.

I have a bad habit of entering a pool where it starts to slow down and widen. It is where the easiest wading is to be found. You'd think I'd learn my lesson, wouldn't you, given enough time and watching plenty of fish hooked and landed upstream from me? Still I wander in where the footing starts to get good. At the Black Rock Pool, it is best to wade out just above the rock, where there is an island (often underwater), then bear upstream, farther and farther, until the river narrows, shallows, and quickens, being only a dozen yards wide there.

It is probably advantageous to give such a pool a little rest, once you've thrashed your way so close to its opposite bank. It needn't be for long, because fish in this situation quiet down quickly and soon are receptive to a fly drawn across their bow.

I used to fish this pool with a sink-tip line. As I said, I am slow to learn. A sink tip will catch fish here, and (knowing this) I suppose it is why I am inclined to sink my fly a little bit. It is entirely unnecessary and probably results in fewer fish being hooked than would occur with a floating line. So now I fight off my natural inclination to descend and gear up immediately with a floating line. Seldom am I sorry. And even after the water slows and deepens, in the manner of all pools, there is no need to go deeper. The fish are keyed to the surface and will continue to move to a fly on top or in Frank Amato's first one inch of water. The question remains, why?

To be sure, there is natural food in our rivers, and more of it in rivers on the East slope of the Cascades. But there is never enough to satisfy a hungry (or feeding) steelhead, even if it were able to utilize it for nourishment. Very seldom will steelhead be found taking caddis or grasshoppers or certain mayflies, and then it is almost as though the fish were obeying some obscure urge to indulge in a feeding frenzy, not knowing what or why they do.

The above statements, admittedly, do not make much sense. They are speculations on why fish take food—or flies, for that matter. The speculations are not important, only a recognition that the description of fish behavior is accurate and fishing for steelhead on top—at certain times of the year, on some rivers—will produce not only good results but results that are superior to sunk-fly fishing.

Back to the Black Rock Pool, as illustration. Aside from its bedrock construction and rocky bottom coated with slick brown algae, it is different from Merlin's Pool, being for one thing twice as long and much narrower. In fact, there are many places along its great length where it shallows and becomes pockety and can be carefully crossed to gain access to the dirt road opposite, which leads to other downstream pools. The pool is ledgy, with a natural rocky outcropping confining it in the manner of an artificial riprap. There are tiny back eddies and, just out from them, slots or pockets created by sunken boulders and sandstone or basaltic ledges. Fish take up temporary lies or resting places along here—more likely at some spots than at others that appear from the wader's perspective to be as well suited. But here again, I am not a steelhead, so I do not know why. The most that I can do is collect observations about where steelhead seem to like to lie and concentrate my fishing activity there.

Fishing this wonderful pool with the floating line offers the fly to fish lying at a variety of stations, some deep, some shallow, some tight to the bank, some practically underfoot. And these fish will move a fair distance to intercept the fly, so the correct presentation at all times during a downstream progression may draw a strike from a fish afar. This is another reason why a surface-working fly is so effective. It draws fish, while a sunk fly usually just appeals to fish in its immediate vicinity during its wide sweep.

If you fish a sink tip in such water, the fly will always go down, and in water that is not deep the fly will be on the bottom much of the time. It will be swept into rocks and become fixed there, necessitating breaking it off; if not firmly snagged, to get it to return to you the line must be tugged hard, and this motion will frighten and put down fish many yards away. It is common for a wet-fly angler to disturb all the fish in his pool and not only reduce his chances of hooking one to near zero but also the chances of everybody immediately following him. This is not good.

A floating-line fisher disturbs nothing, nobody, not if he is careful to lift his line off and lay it down quietly on water that is likely to hold resting fish. What he does not hook, he leaves in a ready state for the next fisher, dry line or wet. It is one reason why wet-fly fishers often invite the dry-line person to go through a pool first. He does them no harm and may actually benefit them by alerting a fish that will later take wet. Of course the dry-line fisher may hook a fish, and it is not pretty to see the response of the sunk liner to this, for he often believes he has given away his advantage.

Fishing such a pool with a floating line allows the angler to vary his presentation from cast to cast, even while using the same fly rigged up the same way. Let us say it is a Bubbleheaded Muddler he is fishing, which goes through the water half-sunk and naturally wriggling some. He can fish it tight line, pulling through a little at the end of the drift, where the water slackens, giving the fly as much action as possible. Or he can fish it with mends providing constant slack to the line, so the fly drifts naturally along and bobs occasionally, struggling a bit, then quieting down, like an injured creature. This is most enticing. And it is fun to do; there is considerable pleasure in making the line and fly behave exactly as you wish them to.

You have an idea in your head about what action it will take, on such a day, on a given river, to bring a rise. You try to approximate this action, reading the river and the surface of the water, applying all the experience from all the rivers of your past. And the odd thing is, a fly on a given run will behave entirely differently from what experience leads you to expect. The currents are subtly and not so subtly different. This brings all your learning to naught. You are a novice again, a beginner.

It is what is meant by the term "born yesterday," only, in this case, it translates "born anew each day."

What usually goes wrong is that the belly does not behave as planned. The current where the belly lies grabs it, or else fails to grab it, and the fly's course is direly affected. The fly either hangs in an eddy, as the belly is whisked downriver until it catches and whips the fly across the run in alarming fashion, or else the belly starts backing up toward you in a near eddy, while the fly bobs along for only a moment before it begins to drag. Either way its behavior is not conducive to a steelhead strike. You make a second cast, slightly differently, and strive for a better result. Of such actions and reactions is your day comprised.

Pockety water such as the Black Rock Pool has a surprisingly even flow throughout its course. After its initial spurt and slowing down, the current fans out, and while the bottom is uneven, the surface is uniform, the current at the fisher's back still strong, and the river bottom shallows gradually until it reaches the near bank some distance away; this means the same cast repeated exactly will produce consistent, predictable results.

If every cast fishes nearly the same way, you may wish to add some variety to them so as not to bore yourself or the fish. A floating line permits this, while a sinking one does not so readily. Often I will slam the fly down hard on its forward cast and draw it toward me with a few sharp tugs; the fly floats, hops, whips, and skates, and sometimes a steelhead will chase it. If I do it just right, and my strike is timed perfectly, I will have a good connect. But there is a tendency to keep fishing the fly hard and take it away from a pursuing fish. Then all you see is a big whirl in the water, as a bathtub is created, and you do not come tight to your fish. You'll have a story to tell at home about the big one that got away. It is only half the truth. The rest is your failure to hook the fish.

If a pool is so long as this one, a pleasant rhythm can be produced by "step-fishing," with a similar cast, or one that is varied only slightly, being made as you progress steadily downstream. This is much like sunk-line fishing. It differs, however, to the extent in which the fly is given small changes in its behavior or action. The smallness may be all that is necessary, from cast to cast, to interest a steelhead today. Moving along a run, every fish in every lie will see your fly to its best advantage. Mostly the fly will be ignored. But there are days—especially on this pool, with moving fish in a freshened river—when many fish come to your fly. It is not the once-in-a-lifetime experience it might seem to be. On this run, it happens numerous times each season.

Once I started in at the top and soon hooked a fish, which I landed. I reentered the water at about the same hooking point and was soon fast to another. I kept reentering at what I thought to be the point where I hooked the last fish. At six fish hooked, landed, and released, I found myself only halfway through the pool, with the day still long and myself having a sore shoulder. So I drove away. How many more taking fish did it contain?

Other fishers I've talked to report as many as a dozen fish hooked or landed on this water—the stories get a little vague and wild at this point. I believe them all. At such times many active fish are about and whoever is present will get his share and more, unless he is doing something very wrong. Usually a floating line works best and interests the maximum number of fish. All the fly has to do is be pitched out there in the center of the run and the fish will provide the rest of the action. A beginner, having such an experience, will think he has mastered the sport. He will soon have his comeuppance. I know one trout fisher (the late Dave Round) who had excellent fishing but never had the urge to return for more. It takes all kinds.

Most of the time what we get is ordinary fishing. This means a fish or two hooked and some, all, or none of them landed. In the course of a long day, good fishing might consist of a couple hooked for eight or ten hours fishing. It might be comprised of some action every two or three hours. It is common knowledge that it takes an average fisher about 30 hours to bring one steelhead to the beach. If this is so, every time we land one more quickly, some poor sap goes all that much longer without one—at least statistically speaking.

And sometimes that poor sap is us. It is why I am supremely grateful for every steelhead I hook and do not require a great number of them in a day or in a season to make me happy.

NINETEEN

One day on the North Fork, late in August, I went out and fished two pools, armed with the dry fly. I had no action, not even from piddlers, not so much as a cutthroat trout, either, until I got to the bottom of my final pool. Then a big fish came twice to my fly and tugged on it hard, with a splash each time, then would come no more. Steelhead, I knew. That is how it goes. Was that a successful evening or not?

Well, it depends on your orientation. To Bob Taylor, back in the Sixties, it was pretty good. To me, today, it is, too. But to many confirmed steelheaders it would be next to nothing. They would scoff. They have higher expectations of the river and themselves. Well, they are doomed to frequent disappointment. Even Lee Wulff took his skunks and was reconciled to them. Remember this.

A trout fisher goes out to stream or lake and rarely returns home without hooking and landing a trout or two. Or three or four or five. This is ordinary fishing. For a trouter to catch nothing takes a big blow or a torrential rainstorm.

A steelheader is often beaten by his favorite stream, but does not damn it to eternity or go elsewhere. He returns, forewarned and mentally armed ahead of time for more disappointment. He does not measure his success in dead fish; well, not often. He soon develops what is called a philosophical outlook; it could also be called resignation. It might be called a religious attitude, too. Zen Buddhism comes close to describing its nature, for it encompasses the absurd but says no action is entirely foolish, not if rightly perceived. Nor is any action ultimately wise.

I'm sure somebody (Jim Vincent, if no other) has already written a Zen tale of steelhead fishing, but I've missed it. Thirty years ago Art Smith turned to me suddenly, after about ten hours of fruitless casting, saying, "Suppose every steelhead we've caught is a fluke?"

I said something like, "You mean, we are all sitting in a dark closet with a thread and a needle, and occasionally we run it through the slot?" "Exactly." "What's your point, Art?" "There is no point. You understand perfectly." I'm not sure that I did or do.

Once Bob Taylor, an early environmentalist and a man who understands the subtle workings of the ecosystem, right down to the last caddis creeper on that rock, told me about the Sierra Club's maxim, "Take only pictures, leave only footprints." It was the first time I had heard it. Of course it is a truism now.

I responded, "Why is it necessary to leave footprints in the sand? If everybody wore felt on his boots, as we do, there would be no footprints. Everything would be perfect." He looked at me peculiarly.

There is something simply wonderful, sublime, about going out to a river, fishing alone (or with a nuisance dog, like Sam), catching a fine steelhead on a fly of your own tying, on the surface, in a manner that may seem unnatural to everybody but a steelhead and you, playing it as well as you are capable, landing it, releasing it, doing a little dance on the beach, singing a snatch of a song you didn't know you remembered, and going on your cheery way. You have no fish to clean, no forensic evidence of your feat, no snapshot, no meat to eat or otherwise dispose of (in the freezer, for instance, the halfway house to the garbage can), no smell on your hands and the steering wheel afterwards; nothing but the memory.

Thanks for the memory.

TWENTY

I am a writer who fishes. Make no mistake about it, the word order is correct. On a given day, with the planning and execution of that day all up to me, I will often elect to write if something is pressing, difficult, or interesting, instead of traveling a distance to go fishing. Friends who do not write envy me, thinking I fish every time I want to. It is not true or accurate. Fishing has to serve as an opportunity, a respite, a reward.

Of course I *choose* to write on a rainy day, when the river has gone out. And I often *decide* to go fishing on a clear, bright day, with a rising barometer and the river dropping and growing greener by the hour. I didn't say there weren't perks to this line of work.

A man who is retired, or self-employed (not the same thing, by the way), will choose to fish at mid-week, if he is smart, and avoid the weekend crowd. My friend, Dake Traphagen, who makes and I suppose plays classical guitars in Bellingham, does this. We are always trying to convince each other of how hard we work when we are not out on the river, frothing it with our fly lines. And we pretend never to believe each other.

Nonetheless it is true. Everybody takes pride in working hard, then rewarding himself with something pleasurable, whether it be a beer, a movie, or going fishing. (I partake of all three often.) And mid-week fishing is great, the crowd is usually down (except at the season's peak, when many take vacation), the fish less disturbed, the illusion of the wilderness experience more likely to be achieved. Those of us who are able to arrange our time thus are lucky, and we know it. But those who must fish weekends hold us in contempt, I know, and I don't blame them. They accuse us of shunning the competition. They say we are unable to compete with them and prevail. It may be true. The only way to know is to put yourself to the test and see how you do. Not once or twice but many times.

It is quite different a situation then. If you arrive on the river at about eleven in the morning, as I often do, you will find you are not the first or second person to go through the pool, this day, but probably the twelfth or fifteenth. Does it matter? Perhaps not, if you can't be the first.

When I first started fishing for summer-run steelhead it was under conditions much worse than today. I never fully forget it. There was a mile of prime water (not twenty miles) and every good angler in the Tacoma-Seattle-Everett corridor made the weekend foray to the North Fork. The lineups were incredible, sometimes stretching down the river and out of sight, men spaced out every fifteen or twenty feet, each of them fishing just about the same way: deeply sunk.

Often when a steelhead struck it seemed totally random. It could be anybody casting a wet fly downstream and across. The fact that it happened to some more than to others was hard to fathom. Of course the lucky ones took full credit. Perhaps they deserved it, but I think it was mostly the luck of the draw. Today it still is. Whenever I see (and participate in) a lineup, I sadly realize my and everybody else's chances are diminished proportionately; that is, according to the number of people going through the water in a similar manner at about the same time.

Usually an advantage can be had by fishing totally differently. Often anglers plumb their pools, believing they can dredge up a fish that nobody else has reached down to. This works just frequently enough to gain adherents. But more likely than not the fish throughout the pool will have been uprooted. They will have been moved out of their lies by lines dragged along the bottom and by flies pulled around rocks in a disturbing manner. They will be moving around the pool and seeking portions of it where these untoward things don't happen, at least not so regularly. And—having moved—they may be on the take. If so, chances are it will be near the surface.

If you watch steelhead in a pool, at first you will be astonished by what you see. They don't behave as you expect them to. Known to disdain sandy lies, you find them lying over sand (though not for long, and usually not when people are around). They tend to be skittish in such water. And they do not lie on the bottom, clinging to their shadows. They lie fairly high up in the water column, their shadows (by which they can be spotted) being a good distance away from their bodies. Occasionally they hold just under the surface and, in a shadowy run with a broken surface and a spot of sunlight, the current constantly rearranging itself, a window will suddenly appear through which you can see a steelhead as clearly as though there were no water in the river, no shadow, no dappled light. Of course your fish can see you, as well, and may move off. Make the slightest abrupt movement and he will be gone in a wink of silver.

This fish may have been once disturbed and certainly will be again. Having been made to go on the move, he may well become a taking fish. It is odd, but true.

On a crowded weekend, with a steady stream of accomplished anglers going through a good pool, there is little opportunity to give the water the half-hour rest you would like it to have. You must join the progression or, at best, enter the water shortly after the last angler has left the pool in disgust at not having hooked anything. This may not be the worst event in the world.

During the week, when you arrive on the same pool at your favorite choice of times, and find nobody pummeling it, it may have been recently abandoned under conditions very much like those found on a weekend, only you don't know so. You presume it to be quasi-virginal. You fish it intently, with confidence, believing what is false. And you hook a fish—not where you expected to hook one, from experience, but in an entirely different place; a real surprise. Then why can't you do it on the weekend? Well, you can.

This is the real test of whether or not you are any good. True, fishing doesn't have to be highly competitive, though there are many who like it no other way, and they can be found fishing happily on Sundays or on everybody's Saturday—usually an even worse day from the standpoint of crowds. If you can't accept it this way, you will have to peel off your neoprenes early, for a mob scene is all that is available to you.

But if you bite your lip and plod through the pool after two or three anglers, you may hit a fish. Surprise. I don't know why it is so, but often the number of fish a pool will put out is in direct proportion to the number of anglers going through it—the more the better. So if you are alone, and only two fishers (let us say) visit a pool in a morning, one of you may hit a fish, but if six or eight fish the pool on a given morning, maybe three or four fish will consent to strike. So why not give the crowd a try? It is better than reading all the Sunday paper or playing golf.

Let's look at it another way. If eight fishers probe the pool and only one fish is hooked, it may be yours. If it is you with the morning fish, you can take full credit, and believe for a short duration that you are as good as you'd like to think you are. And if you don't get the fish, you can blame it on the mob scene.

Another trick that may work, if you only have weekends to fish, is using the VCR. The Good Lord made VCRs for steelhead fly fishers, for the televised football games of September and October are played just when fishing is best. Men who like both steelhead and football are thrown into a quandary. Fish or watch the organized brutality? The availability of the VCR says you can do both.

It is a wonder that all fishing/football lovers don't avail themselves of this simple device. Many believe the VCR is solely to watch rented movies on. This may be a corollary of the widely held belief that most people—men included—don't know how to program a VCR timer, or have screwed up so badly the few times they have tried as not to want to try again. Well, anybody who has learned how to tie a simple wet fly from a book can read the VCR instruction manual and make the machine behave.

All this is so obvious as to probably not need stating, yet during a key football game, rivers are often deserted. It is amazing how many men believe that all televised football games are played for their real-time personal benefit. The good news is, roll will not be taken. So time your weekend sorties for game time, and watch the contest only after the sun goes down.

Twenty-one

Last year I got off to a good start on the Wenatchee, with a big early fish on the surface at the end of August. It was wild, so I put it back. A few days later, fishing under the lower Monitor Bridge, I hooked another fine fish that took just under the surface in a run of slab rock and raced nearly a hundred yards downstream to the bridge abutment, where it jumped as high as my head.

Backing line was strewn all over the river, and I hurried to gather it on the spool again, which was of small diameter and required many turns. Finally the fish came under control, but not before a series of delightful runs and jumps. Steve McCurdy of the Fish and Wildlife Department came down and watched me land it. It was a hatchery fish, a female of about eleven pounds. Steve said it was the brightest Upper Columbia fish he had ever seen. I proudly agreed (though I deserved no credit for this). He wanted to take some scale samples. Scale samples from a hatchery fish, I wondered? I asked, "What for?" They were doing a survey, he explained shortly. But weren't most hatchery fish much the same? Same year class, or the one just before it? All in the six-to-twelve-pound range? Yes, he said, but added no more.

I told him I was more interested in the wild fish, fish that had spawned in the river, spent some indeterminate length of time there as juveniles, then went to sea for another unknown period. These, I knew, varied greatly. Some fish are small, some that friends and I had been catching for several years were quite big—sixteen and seventeen pounders.

He had his instructions, he said. He scraped a dozen scales off my fish and put them in a little manila envelope, on which he recorded the pertinent data. They were all from the fish's side, high up.

"Here," he said, handing me some spare envelopes. "You might save me the scales from your hatchery fish." He presumed I killed them all, which was legal now during the selective fishing season of September and October, for the first time in recent history. This opportunity put a new emphasis on people fishing the Wenatchee early, for in the past hatchery fish couldn't be kept until November first, a time when many of us from the West side had abandoned the river, partly because of snow accumulating in the passes and partly because we did not like to participate in a kill fishery.

I needed a fish now, or rather my wife did. And I had a debt to pay to a couple of orchard owners who had been kind to me and had put in requests. So I killed this steelhead with a few crisp blows to the head with a piece of applewood Steve handed me. Then I cleaned the fish in the river. So bright, I had thought it a male, but Steve said it was a female. He was right. The eggs were larger than I expected from the fish's color; I always forget that ripeness is dependent on time of the year, not coloration. Though the fish would not spawn until April of the following year, the egg masses were already building.

Merlin's Pool

How strange it was to walk away from the Wenatchee with a fish trailing from my fingertips, its tail dragging on the sand.

A few days later I was fishing Merlin's Pool, when I was greeted by Steve on the high bank opposite, where there is a wide pull-off of the highway. Immediately a good fish hit and was off to the races. I followed it downstream under a bright sun that quickly sweated me. The fish, a big male, was slow to come to my side of the river and the spot I had in mind to land him. He kept running back to the center with a strength that told me not to try to check him. But finally he got on the short line and I could lead him around a little, though he always headed away from the patch where I intended to beach (and release) him. I had to settle for another place, one smaller and less to my liking.

I could see the fish's big adipose and broad speckled back. It was wild and about sixteen pounds. It was a wonderful fish, and I was glad to have Steve present, if for no other reason than as a witness. "Big wild fish," I called out, across the river, during a pause in the vehicular traffic noise. "Want some scales?" "No."

I twisted the hook free, righted the fish, and watched it swim slowly back to the center of the river. With my eyes (and my dog, Sam's) fixed on its dorsal, I could see it clearly until it was swallowed up by six feet of water.

I returned to the top of the run and Sam to his sandy patch in the sun, where he approximated sleeping. Always, though, he kept one eye slit for the sight of a taking fish. But we hooked no more fish that September day.

I started thinking about the Wenatchee's wild steelhead run. If Fish and Wildlife wasn't interested in data about them or reading their scales, I was. Why didn't I collect scales on my own? For instance, this big fish I had just released—what would its scales tell me about its life in the river and its time at sea? I would never know, for it was too late to ask the fish to provide me with a viewable sample.

My next fish, however, I was prepared for. It too was big—about fourteen pounds, a male again. Steve had told me to take scales from above the lateral line and behind the dorsal of my hatchery fish. Later I found that I got better-looking scales from slightly in front of the dorsal and more of them proved readable, so I had to take fewer of them: three or four, instead of six or eight. Since I was putting all my fish back now, I wanted to make it as easy as I could on them and reduce the chance of infection, which is always present, especially in a warm river.

I slipped the scales into a Ziploc clear plastic bag of the smallest size I could buy at a hobby store and squeezed the air out of it, retaining a small bit of moisture in the form of slime, which I knew would not evaporate if I zipped the bag completely closed. The moisture would keep the scale from badly drying out and curling. I did not want it to curl because I needed it to stay flat so that it would be in focus when I viewed it through some magnifying device. I did not know what I would use, but I knew enough about optics to understand that the depth of field would be shallow—no more than a millimeter or two. To count rings and to read seasonal cycles, the scale had to be razor sharp.

Numero uno, I thought, filing the bag in an upper vest pocket.

Would I take scales from all the wild fish I caught—a few or many? What were my guidelines? Having taken one set of scales, I had to consider the future, for I was started on a project.

I decided—unlike Wildlife—I wanted atypical fish. Fish in the range of hatchery steelhead, with predictable terms of sea-feeding, did not interest me. Thus, I did not want scales from fish in the six-to- twelve-pound range; just the opposite. Small fish and large fish, to be sure. So to qualify, my fish had to be under six pounds or over twelve.

When I told Steve what I was doing, he seemed ambivalent. No, he seemed disapproving. But he also looked interested. I gathered that he and his bosses had an institutional dislike of lay persons (non-fish biologists, that is) taking scale samples from *their* fish, but there was no specific regulation forbidding it. Hence, the professional frown.

This bothered me not at all, for I knew what I was doing. I had read a few scales before and had a fishing friend who had read a whole lot more. This was Tom Crawford. True, he didn't work for Fish and Wildlife, but he had a masters degree in fish biology, with an emphasis in salmonids. He worked a few months out of the year as a commercial fisher with his own boat that targeted the Bristol Bay sockeye explosion, did biological work on contract for the feds, and fished steelhead for fun the rest of the year. (A good life, isn't it?)

Tom had turned me on to this river and the Sauk, and I owed him an unpayable debt. Back in Seattle (I was journeying back and forth to fish the river at mid-week and was in town to write on weekends), I gave him a call at his home outside of Granite Falls and told him my plan. He was enthusiastic. I explained about my newly formed guidelines. "Very good," he said. "I'll collect scales, too." "Will you help me read them?" "You bet." So began our first year of Wenatchee River wild-steelhead scale sampling.

We didn't collect a whole lot, namely because there were quite a few hatchery fish in the river and many of the wild fish didn't fit our template. As a matter of fact, we got only six. (Fishing with Sam, sometimes it is necessary to decide to pass up a sample, rather than subject the fish to a dog-battering.) But six is a start. Six is a sample. Six is enough to detect a trend, however small. But six will not do for scientific purposes. You need many, many fish and scales. We will never have enough, not even if we fished everyday, both of us, and had phenomenal luck, which of course is what we would like to do.

We had to settle for occasional trips at mid-week throughout the season, which is roughly two months long. We gathered what came to us and were grateful. I found a way to project the scales with a library microfiche viewer and dupe them with a copier that comes attached to the viewer at Seattle Public Library. (The fact that my wife, Norma, is a librarian in the system didn't hurt my case any, though the librarian in the department says she will cooperate with anybody who respects the equipment.)

So I now have prints from scales of six wild Wenatchee steelhead that, I am positive, were not seriously injured and all lived to spawn. The longest a fish of ours has remained at sea is a little over three years. The shortest is one. The data is provisional, of course, and based on a tiny sample. It indicates that our fish lived in the river for two years after they were hatched—not in a hatchery tray but in the gravel of the river bottom.

They were not fed a diet of Oregon moist pellets but foraged on what they found naturally—a fair abundance of riverine insect life. The foraging made them muscular and quick. They grew over their long, first summer and became inactive when the river cooled, then turned frigid. In spring, they began to feed

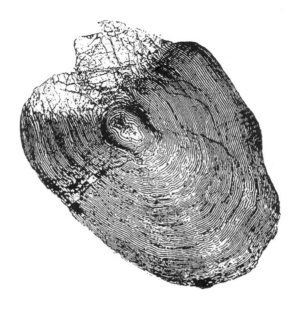

Wild fish scale, 14 pounds (Wenatchee River).

again, and were about four inches in size and prettily spotted. Wenatchee river fish tend toward a deep rainbow coloration and keep it until they smolt; these hues blend in well with the brown silt and algae of the river bottom.

The second year they were equally aggressive and able to consume more food because of their greater size. It was important for them to achieve good growth because in the spring—if they were big enough—they would smolt; if not, they remained in the river a third year and endured another Wenatchee winter. (Nobody, given a choice, would do that, not even a fish. Smart young steelhead would follow the orchardists south to Arizona and New Mexico.) They ate whatever bugs they found in the adult or larval stages, feeding hungrily and not too selectively.

Then the second winter arrived and they went into hibernation. They ate naught and some burrowed into the gravel when the river became turbid and discolored. In spring, with the return of long daylight hours and warmer water, they underwent the great transformation that enabled them to live in the salty sea and grow large. They collected themselves into schools of smolts and began their migrations through the great, slow reservoirs that stretch between the dams on the Columbia. The losses at each reservoir and dam were great. Only a fraction survived.

Others were lost at sea. They ranged as far off as the Asian coast. They followed their forage fish, including schools of squid and elvers. They grew and grew. Then it was time to head back to the Columbia. My scales led me to conclude that different year classes of adult steelhead became mixed and schools and runs formed of genetically varied fish, wild and hatchery, all headed for the same rivers. They came to Bonneville, the Dalles, John Day, McNary, and at each dam some adults didn't make it. Eventually they reached Rock Island Dam and, just above it, the slow deep mouth of the Wenatchee. There they remained, venturing forth into the river's slack, then dropping back into the Columbia, waiting for the irrigation diversion to end, the water to cool, themselves to feel the urge to ascend. And then we caught some of them.

Of course the scales told me considerably less than all this; much of it I already knew. But in the instance of each scale I could see variations on the same theme. The dark ragged band between evenly spaced rings indicated winter non-feeding months. I looked for the tight jagged line that indicated a spawning fish that had survived its maiden effort, but could find none. It is always the hope against hope, in the Snake or Columbia fishery, to come across a steelhead that has survived and gotten past all those dams again to return to sea and meet the challenge of ascending the dams a nearly impossible second time to spawn. One looks and looks, wishing it to be so, and is always disappointed. But maybe some day, *one* such fish will be found. I should like to be the one to do it.

Much later in the game I learned from a Dick Teske article that 60 percent of the wild steelhead return after two years at sea, while 60 percent of the hatchery fish spend only one year at sea. My own information supports this, with the wild fish being bigger, especially late in the year. Back during the construction of Grand Coulee Dam, fearing a loss of wild stock in the upper Columbia system, steelhead were trapped at Rock Island Dam near Wenatchee and indiscriminately distributed throughout the system, in hopes of saving as many fish as possible. Starting in 1962, fish were trapped at Priest Rapids Dam instead; they came from many different Columbia stocks. Hatchery employees took whatever they could find.

Since 1984, however, stock for the Wenatchee has come from traps at Wells Dam, far upstream. Most are hatchery fish. Fish Biologist Larry Brown estimates that maybe 10 percent are wild, but even the wild are progeny of hatchery fish that have spawned in the river. The good news from all of this is that the brood stock captured for about 45 years was obtained from the Columbia system and is indigenous. The bad news is that the stock has a

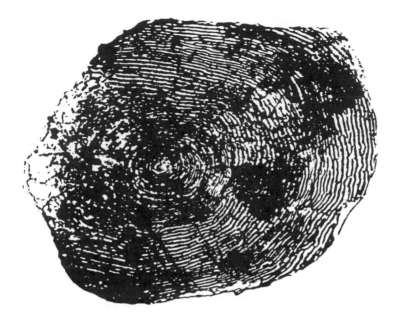

Hatchery fish scale, six pounds (Wenatchee River).

hatchery origin and its genetics are self-perpetuating. Accordingly, the fish do not have a broad genetic diversity and may be more susceptible to disease and ravaging from natural disasters, such as the Great Flood of 1990, which seems to have taken its toll.

Wild fish are important; they will survive if the hatchery component gets devastated (as seems to happen, more and more often) by disease, natural events, or mechanical failure in hatcheries. Collecting scales from wild fish can tell us a lot about their life cycle and individual differences among fish. Next year Tom and I intend to continue our experiment. "For the sake of science," we will strive to catch as many wild steelhead as we can, big and little. This is fun in itself. We will treat them gently, respectfully, lovingly, for they represent the future of the race. We plan to invite other responsible fishers to participate in our survey, for we need as much data as possible. We feel the need of at least three consecutive years of gathering data to make any sense out of what we find, for the shortest life cycle of a wild steelhead is that number of years. There are worse ways I can think of to spend one's autumn.

When I decided to start collecting scales I realized I didn't know much about them, although I had looked at quite a few scales by that time, many of them in books. I decided to try to learn more about them through further reading. Each scale contains the life history of that particular fish, starting from the time it is a free-swimming fry and continuing to record its growth until its life is terminated, usually by some fisher. Its history exists in the form of growth rings, rings not unlike (in appearance, anyway) the rings on a tree. But whereas a tree puts on one growth ring for each year, a fish puts on numerous, and the distance between individual rings indicates the amount of feeding the fish has done. Thus, in a steelhead's river life, the rings are close together, as the food supply is limited in a rich river, even for a hungry parr. In saltwater, food is abundant most of the year and the growth rings are widely spaced out, reflecting how quickly the fish is putting on weight. Yet in winter, both in rivers and the sea, the food supply falls off sharply, and this is information recorded on the scale and evidenced by a narrowing of the bands until they practically pile atop each other. When a steelhead enters a river to spawn, it stops feeding and there is no more growth for a long time—up to eleven months for summer runs. Often there is great deterioration of the fish during its spawning cycle and, in addition to its lack of feeding, the rigors of spawning are indicated in considerable degradation of the scale; until the fish returns to saltwater the scale does not begin to regenerate and show the widely spaced bands that come from rich feeding in the sea.

This deterioration is called a spawning mark. Spawning marks resemble the natural cessation of feeding that occurs winters in both river life and in the sea, but are much more ragged and ravaged looking. Often a jagged black band is produced that circles the scale, and there may be white patches, here and there. A.H.E. Wood—of greased-line fame—used to carry a low-powered microscope in his fishing bag and would take a scale from an "interesting" fish to examine, mainly to see if it had spawned once or twice already. According to his biographer, Jock Scott, he advised us to do the same, if we want to know more about our fish.

Of course there is no reason for a steelhead to leave the saltwater except to spawn, so any time the fish stops feeding for long a spawning mark should be looked for. In time, after viewing many scales, the difference between what is called a check, or a winter band, and a spawning mark can be discerned. Oddly, there is a small summer band or check that occurs in many fish around July, when a shortage of food in saltwater is reflected in a narrowing of the growth rings. Nobody has been able to explain this satisfactorily to me.

If each winter there is a scarcity of food in both fresh and saltwater, this is an indication on the scale that one year has passed. Most wild steelhead spend almost two years as fry and parr before they smolt and leave for the sea. As might be expected, these two winters can easily be seen in what is called the river nucleus of steelhead (and coho salmon). The winters spent at sea show up clearly, too, and indicate a fish's additional years. In a few odd cases, and as one travels northward into Canada and Alaska, steelhead parr spend longer in their rivers before they achieve enough growth to become smolts; these additional years show up on the river nucleus. Three-year-old and four-year-old parr are exceptions down here, however. And a hatchery smolt will show one year of great growth, with no winter band and wider-than-expected growth rings.

Stillaguamish River hatchery fish, five pounds.

A Deer Creek summer-run steelhead shows growth rings typical of a wild fish. Here is the two-year river nucleus, with its tight, narrow bands showing its growth to smolt-size over two summers. After its second winter in freshwater, the rings quickly widen out and indicate sudden greater growth. There is a single narrowing series of bands that indicates the first winter spent in the ocean. The fish is now three years old. Following the third winter, abundant sea feeding is resumed again, as the fish heads for its river mouth, where it transitions biologically (in a process the opposite of smolting) to life in freshwater again; part of this change is adapting to a salt-free environment and losing the capability of benefitting from food. Even in

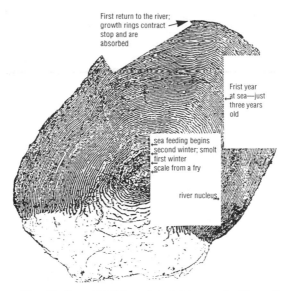

First return to the river; growth rings contract stop and are absorbed

Frist year at sea—just three years old

sea feeding begins
second winter; smolt
first winter
scale from a fry

river nucleus

Detail of a wild fish scale, eight pounds (Deer Creek).

freshwater, the bands continue to form, but are bunched, dark, and irregular, for no food is being consumed; instead, fat and protein are being converted into energy and the development of milts or roe. These narrow bands are formed just under the scale's outer layer.

Most wild summer runs are three years old, if their internal processes have not been altered by genetic mixing with hatchery fish.

Hatchery stock is often chosen for its early-return trait, that is, fish ascending in early spring instead of mid-summer, and for its unusual two- and three-year sea-feeding characteristics. These fish are not typical of summer runs, though fishers like them because they are so big. (This is more likely to be true for Skamania stock than for fish trapped in the upper Columbia River system.) These genetic traits are reproduced in the so-called wild fish returning from hatchery plants spawning naturally in our rivers. Given enough time and sufficient spawning habitat, they tend to dominate and drive out the wild component of the run. Consequently, we are now getting much bigger summer fish in our rivers, because they are programmed to stay at sea longer; the trade-off, however, is in loss of genetic diversity and perhaps in the stock's resistance to disease.

The scales Tom and I collected the first year show most fish had a two-year river life, followed by less than two years at sea. Since the fish feed continuously in saltwater, the time in spring or summer when they enter the river to some extent governs their size. A fish may add a pound or more to its weight between, say, May and August. Young fish are of slightly different size as smolts when they enter the salt, which may account for how much food they can utilize out of the sea's abundance. Thus, the different sized adults in a year's run.

Most very large steelhead prove to be first-time spawners. They may be five or six years old, according to their scales. The relationship of river life to life in the sea is expressed by fish biologists as river years separated from ocean years by a slash, eg. 2/2, for instance, with the first 2 being two years in the river, followed by the second 2 indicating two years at sea. A less than full year is not counted; hence the use of "plus" in describing a young fish's river life.

Deer Creek wild summer-runs are invariably 2/1 fish; I cannot stretch them into having spent a second year at sea, and they are hardly ever over 30 inches in length or ten pounds in weight. My top two wild fish from the Stilly are just over eleven pounds each and are separated by many years. One I killed, one I didn't.

The shortest life cycle of a mature wild steelhead appears to be three years. Hatchery summer runs often dwarf them. They are 1/2 or 1/3 and sometimes even 1/4 or 1/5 fish, and some will nudge the 20-pound mark. This puts the fish into the trophy class.

But I am getting far afield. My subject is the floating line and flies that for the most part float.

TWENTY-TWO

D ry-fly design is one of the many good things that can be traced to Lee Wulff. It goes back to the days of the Great Depression and the year in which I was born, it so happens. Lee was fishing with Dan Bailey—whom history indicates was more of a promoter and tester than an originator of fly patterns.

Anyway, in that year Lee and Bailey were fishing together often, and the fishing was good. They started out in the streams of New York state—where Lee had always had his home. The Beaverkill and Ausable were two

Lee Wulff

favorites, and the men did a fair amount of damage to the trout population, for food was scarce and this was long before the days when fishers could afford the luxury of putting fish back. They also made forays to the Nipigon—giant brook-trout country.

The dry flies of their day did not float well. They had stiff hackle fibers for tails and wings made of various materials, mostly feathers from game-cocks and ducks. These absorbed water readily and the flies had to be repeatedly clipped off leaders, dried, and regreased. It was more than an annoyance; it was a detriment, especially when a hatch was on and the trout were rising like fury. A minute or two lost was the difference between a fish or two hooked or not. Then often the hatch was over, and with it the fishing for the day. And the fishing was excellent, the trout big.

Lee was an engineer by training and a Stanford graduate who had decided not to practice his trade but instead try different ways to make his living. For a while he was an illustrator and commercial artist, but times were bad and there were no more jobs in this area than in others. To pass the time, he fished. He and Bailey went out to the rivers every chance they got, and camped and fished. Lee started his search for natural materials that would float a hook better than greased chicken feathers. Deer hair was hollow and trapped air in the core that supported it, even when doused a few times. Bucktail of the white-tailed deer proved best, though calf too was good. He began the experiments that led to the development of the Wulff series of flies and writes that he would have given them less egocentric names, except Bailey urged him not to for commercial purposes.

Lee says, "Otherwise I would have named them Ausable Gray, the Coffin May, and the Bucktail Coachman. Dan, then a teacher at Brooklyn Polytechnic Institute, was getting deeply into commercial fly tying. We sat down to work out a greater series of patterns so that he'd be able to sell more of this new type of dry fly. I had already planned a Grizzly pattern because of my success with the Grizzly King in my western fishing. Dan and I worked on to bring out a Blonde, a Brown, a Black, and the rest of the ten patterns he listed for sale."

At the time Ray Bergman was writing his epic *Trout* and he listed the patterns. Lee says the flies were the only ones in the book that were comprised of animal hair instead of feathers. He goes on to add, "I have a letter from Ken Lockwood, who made the gray Wulff into the Irresistible" by adding a clipped deer hair body to it—an important innovation. Lee says his own flies "opened up the way for the Humpy, the Rat-Faced, and the rest of the other-than-feather flies." [Page 71, *The Complete Lee Wulff*, abstracted from his article, "Some Flies I've Designed and Fish With."]

As nearly as I can tell, this was the genesis of the modern dry fly. Much that is effective today stems from this fertile period, 1929-1932.

Dan Bailey found the dressing for Don Gapen's Muddler Minnow about 1936 or 1937 and popularized it, as he had the Wulff series a few years earlier. He was now living in Livingston, Montana, where the deer-haired flies proved just as effective on Western cutthroats and rainbows as they had on eastern brookies and browns.

What was so great about the Wulff innovations was that they were simply flies of several basic colors that floated excellently and—tied correctly—were next to indestructible. Instead of coming apart as a result of hooking many trout, the fly tends to thin down and become even more effective. And if it gets all slimied up, it will ride low in the water and still continue to catch fish. It is a wonderful style and continues to serve us well. It is also inexpensive to tie, for deer remain plentiful and the tail furnishes both the brilliant white for the wings (the white is enhanced through a cleaning process and becomes daylight fluorescent from modern detergents) and a good rich brown.

If the lineage I've just traced goes from Wulff to Bailey and Bailey to Gapen and back again to Bailey, there may be a link between the muddler and the Wulff series, and if there isn't, the common use of deer hair connects the flies, anyway. The fact that Bailey was tying both kinds and selling them for 50 percent more than other tyers got is testimony to their effectiveness.

From this parentage can be traced most of the modern dry flies in use today.

The Thirties weren't all so long ago. On the West Coast anglers were tying sinking flies also of bucktail—flies mostly with a backward-pointing white wing. Hair had a naturally floating quality, which was not desired and had to be defeated for wet-fly purposes. With old-fashioned silk lines, it was difficult to do. Steelhead anglers had to weight their flies in order to fight against the buoyant quality of the materials and lines had to be encouraged to sink, for they were manufactured to be treated and float.

I think it was more of a coincidence that bucktail was the common element than the result of any intelligent planning. But when Western anglers began to float their flies for summer steelhead, at first they abandoned the bucktails they had been using and reverted to heavily hackled flies. This made absolutely no sense and was self-defeating. Lee Wulff pointed this out to them the way he always did—by example. He outfished them with his new flies.

Wulffs and muddlers form the core for today's surface fishing. And the other flies Lee mentions, such as the Rat-Faced McDougal and Irresistible, were the first dry flies I had much success with. I, along with other anglers of my time, were fishing trout-styled dries, the best of which were Royal Coachman, Double-Gray Hackle, Purple Peril; and when sea-run cutthroats were in the river, along with steelhead, we used brighter flies that had been originated to attract brookies, like Paramachene Belle and Beau, Montreal, Grizzly King and Queen, McGinty, etc.

I think many of these flies developed Wulff-style dressings in the Forties and Fifties and thus floated better. I tied the Purple Peril Wulff-style and found that it floats and fishes much better than the sloppy Montreal wet it started out to be.

Similarly, the great sea-run cutthroat fly, Conway Special, is much like a Paramachene Belle and may have been derived from it. A touch of yellow helps for cutts. There is a direct relationship between Haig-Brown's Steelhead Bee to McGinty and the Western Bee; the style of Haig-Brown's bee goes in the direction of a Wulff, but with one notable exception: it is intended to float low in the water, and the way the wing tips forward will riffle it naturally. Plus the materials of tail and wing, fox squirrel, soak up water quickly. Even dressed with mucilin or Silicote, squirrel soon takes on water and rides low, which is what it was intended to do. (Note: if your Steelhead Bee keeps sinking, don't worry about it; a false cast or two will dry it off just enough to float on a slack line, and when it starts to go under again, it is doing what it was intended to do. If it truly sinks, it isn't going to go very deep on a floating line, anyway.)

I make such a case for Lee Wulff's flies because I've caught so many fish on them, and when I depart from his dressings, I still head off in the direction he indicated. I think it is only fair that we acknowledge our sources, rather than make a foolish and unsubstantial case for our originality. Most new flies—wet or dry—are highly derivative.

I'm not sure I know the difference between the dressings for the Rat-Faced McDougal or Irresistible, or care enough to go back to the textbooks to search them out. It doesn't much matter. When steelheaders sit down for an evening's tying, we usually work by designation and feel, using whatever materials are at hand and knowing ahead of time whether they will float well or little, depending on what effect we are after.

Gapen and Bailey's use of tinsel bodies and oak turkey wings and soft tails of more turkey cause the fly to ride low in the water—much the same way as the fox squirrel in Haig-Brown's bee fly. This is an important departure. It indicates that there comes a time when a surface fly is more productive if it doesn't float high and cockily, but rides low, as if half-drowned. More steelhead are caught by low-riding "dry" flies than by those that float high, I suspect. It is also because so many more anglers now fish them that way—either intentionally or by accident.

The chief differences between the Wulff series of flies and the Gapen muddler are two. One is the long, slim half-sunk silhouette the muddler presents to the fish; the other is its bubble head. The clipped deer-hair head of the muddler is important, both to its overall shape and to its behavior in the water. It causes the fly to bob and dip in the current. Yes, this is another way to say riffle or wake.

The riffling or waking fly (one tied intentionally to do so and not requiring hitches thrown over the eye of the hook) has its ruff as its most important characteristic and that feature has been copied often. Most of today's steelhead dries have some such element. The muddler is different in that its bubble head is fairly unobtrusive. This means the fly can be fished wet—deep or shallow—without great distortion of its intended purpose. Its style allows for all sorts of variations in color; muddlers in purple, orange, red, yellow are effective. Many incorporate marabou in place of or in addition to oak turkey, bringing in yet another taking element.

Flies have their period of vogue, then slipslide into oblivion. Perhaps the most popular steelhead dry fly today is the Bomber. I am less impressed with it than some people because I dispute its claim to be anything new or different. I think its value lies in being a direct descendant of the Wulffs and Irresistibles, plus the muddlers, but not performing any better than what came before it. Trey Combs finds a predecessor in a fly called the Bottle Washer, which in turn seems to be a descendant of the Bi-Visible. Both had densely wrapped hackles the length of the body. The advantage of the Bi-Visible was the white hackle wrapped on after the others—the others were usually brown, sometimes gray. The white helped them be seen in broken water.

The Bomber was one of several flies developed on the Miramichi during the Sixties. It contains the clipped, tapered deer-hair body of the Rat-Faced and the Irresistible, but adds a sparsely palmered hackle. (This is optional.) Most important is a buoyant tail, usually of calf, and a wing to match; the wing is tied tipped forward and acts almost as an extension of the shank of the hook. The wing tends to obscure the eye of the fly and—if it is the usual light-wire upturned eye hook—makes it difficult to tie to the leader. The tail supports the fly, while the wing is intended to plane; tied in such a manner, it is almost impossible to stop the fly from waking, except when it is fished with a slack line upstream.

Combs and others trace the Bomber back to about 1967 on the Miramichi and to a Father Eugene Smith, who popularized it. It was brought West by some visiting anglers, who gave it to Steve Petit and Keith Stonebreaker in Lewiston, Idaho, and they in turn showed it to Bill McMillan, who continued its course Westward to Camas, Vancouver (Washington), and Portland (Oregon). To McMillan this was a very important event and he advanced its popularity and brought it to the attention of fly shops and fly tyers, where its fame spread fast.

Bill caught a lot of steelhead on it, as have other anglers. In fact, there are many who fish only the Bomber during the extended summer season and up until the water everywhere is too cold for fishing on the surface. Other anglers see it more as a locator fly, one to use to search for steelhead and get them excited. Then, they believe, some other fly will produce the take with which the fish is solidly hooked and, they hope, landed. Often it is a wet or sub-surface fly.

This would indicate that fish often come short to the Bomber, or can be said to "play around" with it, but do not always take it solidly, not once or during any number of rises that are often splashy and sensational. This is displeasing to me.

Once on the Wenatchee, when it was turning cold and the river was high from rain and the ending (at last!) of the irrigation diversion, I ran into a young man who was ecstatic about his luck with the Bomber. It was Charlie DeJong. He had fished it hard all day, with no results, but in the evening, just before dark, fishing the swollen Park Drift, a steelhead had come to his Bomber *eight* times.

It was exciting, each strike a thrill, no matter if it did not result in a hooked fish. The conditions were most difficult. Charlie kept putting the fly back to the fish and the fish kept rising and bunting it. Finally he had hooked and landed the fish.

I met Charlie the next day and his enthusiasm had not waned. It was quite a feat. He had started out to do something "pure" and difficult. He had kept at it. He had not wavered in his determination, and he had succeeded.

I, less pure, not so determined, switched over to wet fly when the river came up and hooked many fish. I will not say how many, for this is no contest, and the methods are not comparable, but there were a lot of fish around, fish rapidly running the river. Charlie's accomplishment is not to be diminished, however, for he did what he set out to do. It took skill and persistence. It took incredible patience. But he would have raised many more fish wet, I believe, and hooked most of them, as I and others were doing.

The Bomber can be tied with or without a palmered hackle. I like it best with one, because it looks more like a fly (and less like a lure). McMillan, I believe, likes it without a hackle. He likes it orange, and Don Roberts swears by it purple. I like it either gray or brown—brown a little better.

But I like Irresistible or Old Rat-Faced more, or Spade, fished up on top, winged.

The recorded chronology of the Bomber bothers me, too. I think West Coast steelhead fishers came of age back in the late Sixties, and the shift in the balance of power with the East Coast has been taking place steadily and irrevocably ever since. As Lee Wulff and Dan Bailey took the deer-haired flies West in the Thirties, the flow reversed its direction and has been going the opposite way ever since. Let me illustrate.

I took my first dry-fly steelhead about 1961. I copied my friends, a few of whom had been pulling off this trick for several years. I got the Rat-Faced McDougal pattern from Art Smith, who was widely read. I aped Art. I fished the Rat-Faced and Irresistible before I fished the Wulff series, but once I discovered them I used them to the exclusion of most others. I learned about the Steelhead Bee from Jerry Wintle, a fellow Canadian of Haig-Brown's, when I beheld what Jerry could do with it. This was a few years later.

The Rat-Faced and Irresistible bear an uncanny resemblance to the Bomber and precede it. Doubtless they influenced its development, but I've never read anywhere that they did or how it happened. The two patterns both contain deer hair that is spun on the body, then clipped. Our hackle was all piled up at the head, but most of it was third-grade grizzly or cheap brown rooster, and it did not float a fly well. The tail and wing were of deer hair, too, but we generally tied our wing pointing up or slightly back. Often the fly would ride along on its nose and struggle. Planing, we soon learned, produced fish. We were literate; we read Wulff and Haig-Brown and emulated them. We had good success with our borrowed flies. We tried the Portland hitch and used it when conditions warranted. We came up with derivative ties each our own.

There are many kissing cousins in this dry-fly family. The Bulkley Mouse (if I've been told the story correctly, and I think I have) was a no-name fly shown to Colin Shadrack as a boy by Curt Kraemer, our resident area fish biologist with Fish and Wildlife. Tied with moose instead of elk, it floats almost as well and becomes the Moose Turd, a dark fly Bill McMillan first tied and loves. Harry Lemire's Greased Liner shares much with all of these flies, as does my Spade variant, Risible, which goes back about as far. Both Harry's and mine were originally black and gray flies, and differed only in the color of their stub wing. (Mine was white.)

I guess my point is that if Easterners can trace their original patterns no farther back than the mid-Sixties, they might find they are variants of Western patterns, for that is about the time steelhead flies came of age. Lee Wulff sent many dries out here with Dan Bailey in the mid-Thirties; they were accepted quickly and went through sly modifications. The fact that *our* flies are evolved from theirs is possibly less important than *theirs* are now derived from ours.

It is less important, that is, once somebody has stated the case.

TWENTY-THREE

Put a hook in a vice, wrap on some black thread, grab in your left hand a goodly chunk of elk hair, and cut off where it joins the hide. Lash firmly to the hook a third of an inch behind the eye. Trim butts off level with the eye. Snake thread under the ruff and finish with the whip knot. Go fish.

Oh, if you want to be fancy you can dye your elk various hot colors—orange, red, yellow, purple. But it's not necessary. If you don't trust your whip-finish knot, you can give it one or more coats of thin lacquer. While you're there, the bottle open, you can coat the trimmed ruff of elk hair with the goop, thereby stiffening it, but this isn't critical. It works well enough untreated.

Here you have a riffling fly. It will catch steelhead nearly anywhere. Its name? It's not important. Size may be, though. Tie it on eights on down to fours. If you use Wilson hooks, and you should, tie it on tens down to sixes; they run one size larger, at the least.

With this fly you need a floating line and a leader that tapers in stages from a big enough butt to turn over the fly (try .023 or .021) to a tippet of, let us say, six pounds. If you fish the Skeena system, make that eight pound. A good eight pound will land any steelhead in America.

The name of the pattern, please? It is the Mouse. Not the infamous Bulkley Mouse? No, it is the Everywhere Mouse. It is the Washougal Mouse, the Wenatchee Mouse, the Kispiox Mouse, the Umpqua Mouse.

It is a fly as good as the Bomber, old Rat-Faced, or the imitation bee and dragonfly flies, lures all designed to wake or riffle, which the Mouse does nicely, too. Another way to look at this pattern is as an Elk Hair Caddis, with a fat body, or a self-body, and a very thick wing.

It makes a fine caddis imitation, by the way, as good as the Golden Caddis, October Caddis, or Sofa Pillow. You can dress it up, vary it, introduce the new sparkling materials into it, and it will continue to work just fine for you. It may not work any better, for it works well as it comes off the bench, without any imagination being applied to its dressing.

Sometimes more is too much. What is the saying, "Keep It Simple, Stupid?" KISS your fly patterns, too.

Dry-fly design is basically a matter of concept. Just as the muddler has a sculpin in mind, it resembles many other bait fish and insects, as well. So does my Spade—just look at it in the water, with its teardrop shape, its natural colors, its darting motion. Flies like these have a generic insect/bait fish configuration; that is, they look like nothing in particular and everything in general. Toss such a fly into swift, shallow water and it will be attacked by every small salmonid in the area. It—along with many dry flies, such as the Adams—are juicy morsels for small fish and are taken without hesitation. Similarly adult fish, steelhead in particular, will take such flies readily, *when* they take flies.

This is not all the time, admittedly. If it were, small fish would not get to be big ones. Yet it happens often enough to make fishing with the floating (or slightly submerged) fly exciting. Most of these flies have important elements in common. Take wings, for instance. There are many ways of winging a fly. The traditional dry-fly design was of paired sections of duck flight feathers, a right and a left, usually white but sometimes lead-colored, that is, gray. Such wings are matched so that their tips turn outward. (A few are matched with an inward turn of the feathers, forming a tented look. I like these better on a wet fly; the cupped wings produce a teardrop shape and water bubbles are formed in the lee of the fly to give it a lifelike appearance.)

Wulff writes that at the time of the publication of Bergman's *Trout*, only Wulff's flies contained hair; all the rest were of feathers. That was soon to change. Flies became winged in several different styles, most with calf or bucktail. The forward-slanting single wing of the Bomber is an extreme example of the specialty wing, a wing designed to be seen and to wake. But often a hair wing is divided similarly, forming the equivalent of matched duck-slip wings. It is important that both sides of the hair wing be the same length and size so the fly will not twist and turn in the air or in the current, which will give it unnatural behavior and can even put a twist in a fine leader.

A hair stacker can be used to even up the length of the wings of a fly. The stacker is nothing more than a small tube with a removable bottom. The one I bought years ago has several-sized tubes that work off the same bottom, enabling wings of different sizes to be formed. The stacker makes sure the tips are all the same lengths and allows the butts to vary and be trimmed off.

There are advantages and disadvantages to hair stackers. They permit a wing to be made without the loss of many individual hairs that happens when you attempt to even out a stack by hand, i.e., drawing out the longer cut hairs and reforming the wing by laying them back along your finger in much the same way you do in forming a tail with hackles. There is less waste with a stacker; however more time is consumed by using an implement rather than your fingers. I believe it is the most practical way of forming a wing.

Hair is not expensive, so it doesn't much matter if some individual hairs are lost in manual stacking, and the stacking device produces an unnatural-looking wing, one that appears synthetic. My advice is, do not use a stacker on a wet fly; on a dry fly (the smaller, the more necessary) a stacker can be useful in creating a low, dense wing that will tie in neatly and not contain the few long hairs that cause the fly to behave in an unruly fashion, in air or water.

A divided hair wing can be varied greatly from one fly to another. The wing can be tipped forward deliberately to wake without a riffling hitch being applied to the fly, or it can be tied "spent," like a real insect, dying or dead, lying on the water. It can also be tipped slightly back, or tipped way back, and fished with sharp jerks, either in the surface film or just under it.

One time I tied up a few such flies in a pattern shown me by Curt

Kraemer. It was a no-named fly tied with fox squirrel, a golden body, and no hackle. The wing was tipped forward and divided. Being tied of such soft materials, the fly did not float well, but was not mean to; it was intended to ride low and wake.

The fox squirrel was so soft and flexible it quickly absorbed a lot of water, even though I had greased it; it soon sank beneath the surface film, which was annoying. Since I had tied up several, I kept changing them, drying them out on the lambswool pad on my vest and rotating them. I would have switched over to another kind of fly, one that stayed dryer, but I had already hooked two fine steelhead on the new pattern and I wanted to keep fishing it.

It was August, with a lot of salmon and wild steelhead in the river. There were also the first sea-run cutthroats. The fox squirrel fly, thoroughly waterlogged and its sodden wings splayed back, had to be retrieved under the surface, once it no longer floated.

The cutthroat just loved it fished this way. The wings had a lot of latent action; stripped slowly or in jerks, they contracted and expanded in the slow water. The trout pursued the fly and over-ran it. They acted as though they had waited their entire lives for a fly just like this one.

A fly without a divided wing will not flex and contract in the water. It will not produce an enticing sub-surface action; hence it will not draw cutthroats.

I have a few Royal Coachmans tied with white calf wings and no hackle; the wings are tied nearly spent and only slightly tipped forward. The tail is brown bucktail. The fly rides along low in the current, its wings extended helplessly. When retrieved, the fly hops. The wings draw back ever so slightly on the strip, then resume their position at near right-angles to the fly's body when the tension is relaxed. The fly draws strikes from whatever young salmonids are in residence.

The use of hair from an Eastern white-tailed deer is a great benefit to all-around fly tying. It used to be just the brilliant white part I used, and the brown backs went unutilized. I did not throw them away, however, even when the white was gone. I stuffed them into plastic bags and stored them. Today I used the brown backs a lot. I tie my Spade fly tails with them, evening out the hairs by hand and not stacking them with a tool. My tails on most Wulffs and Purple Perils are made from this material too, which is a richer color than deer-body hair or elk. It is not so brittle and does not break off its tips during a normal day's fishing. But it needs to be greased to float.

Also, when a bucktail is dyed any of the usual bright colors required for steelhead fishing, the backs turn an interesting shade. They remain brown, but take on the cast of the dyed color. At the edges of the backside there is a mix of colors, with the brown less dominant, but at the top of the tail, where the brown is darkest, only a small amount of the dye takes hold. This is exactly the right shade to complement other colors and can often be spotted easily in broken water, when you wish to avoid white but do not want to move in the direction of some brilliantly artificial color.

An orange-dyed bucktail has many tones of brown/orange that are wonderful for late-fall fishing when there are big caddis around. Additionally these flies simulate stoneflies—both adults and nymphs.

All this talk about imitating naturals is generally a mistake. The steelhead fly fisher does not need to tell a *Trico* from a *Betis,* an imago from a subimago. Our fish are not normally feeders. It is possible to pursue steelhead, all of your life, and never see them actively feeding. It is also possible to find them feeding fairly often on certain rivers to the East. A steelhead fly is—with a few exceptions—an attractor. Its job is to catch the steelhead's attention and motivate the fish to intercept it.

The few exceptions to the rule of attractors are mostly terrestrial insects, which are incidental to river life. Even if steelhead do not regularly feed, they are known to take the odd bug. A terrestrial is simply a land-born insect that happens to fall into the river and get swept along. These include bees, wasps, grasshoppers, flying ants, etc.; there are damsel and dragonflies, too. There are numerous artificial flies designed to imitate these insects and the flies just happen to be good attractors. It is a happy combination.

However, most floating flies resemble nothing that is found floating on the river. Nobody ever says, "There was a nice hatch of Orange Bombers today on the Grande Ronde," or, "The Wenatchee fish can be found rising to Purple Perils in their imago stage." More likely somebody will say, "I was fishing this great red mother, waking it like crazy, and this dumb steelhead came out of nowhere and sucked it in. Boy, I couldn't have missed." *That* I will believe.

If a steelhead dry is purely an attractor (or is ninety-six percent of the time), then anything goes in color or design. With this idea in mind, I would like to suggest a few exercises of the kind found after chapters in a high school textbook. They are lessons intended to provoke thought, but they produce flies that will take steelhead under various circumstances. (Notice how I hedge.)

1. Tie the Skykomish Sunrise as a dry fly. Keep it small and fish it when there are sea-run cutthroats around. Some tips: for the tail, mix (in a stacker) red and yellow bucktail. Do not use chenille for the body, but try seal or artificial dubbing, bright red, with no fluorescence. Hackles, as with the tail, are to be mixed and can be either soft or stiff; try them both ways. For the wing, do not use polar bear (as the McLeods do for wets) but calf, just this once.

Tie up a few as skaters, too. This means long stiff hackles.

2. There are certain flies that avail themselves of what I call the Generic Spade Design. These include the Boss, the Comet series, Brindle Bugs, and Sack or Burlap flies. (See Fly Plate Number 2.) Tie these as dry flies, with the wing matching the tail in color and material. Burlap strands are okay for the body of the Burlap, but for Brindle Bugs avoid chenille and use your imagination. It is supposed to be variegated, yellow and black. Remember that you don't want it to absorb water, but if the tail and wing float, you can get away with a little body absorption.

If you have real seal in an appropriate color, for Pete's sake use it now. That wonderful shade of Fiery Brown is excellent, and so is hot orange. Put both in a blender. Mix up your generic dries in this style of tie, but remember some will be hard to see in bad light or bright sun. (Move on to 3, without a pause.)

3. Tie a drab dry fly, such as the Spade, then add a sparse wing of brittle white bucktail or bleached deer-body hair. Keep the wing short, very short. Grease it well and start to fish it. Start breaking away the white wing with your thumbnail or your leader cutters until you can still just see it. Keep fishing until you nail a steelhead, alternating patterns and breaking off wing material until you do, or until you lose faith.

4. On a dry line and fairly long leader, tie on your smallest conventional wet fly, such as the Green-butted Skunk, Coal Car, or Fall Favorite. Now add two riffling hitches at the head. Experiment with which side of the head the hitches are turned to, or else tie them directly below the head—that is, in the middle. The latter causes the fly to ride very high in the surface film and draw attention to itself. Fish as you would any waking fly. When a steelhead strikes, try to react slowly. The best way I've found to do this is to disbelieve that you have had a strike and "check" to see if your fly is still on the end of the leader. Often the fish will be well hooked in this length of time. (P.S. I think it takes about three seconds.)

5. Try tying the Skykomish Sunrise with an orange hackle in place of the red, so the mix is orange/yellow—both tail and hackle; the body can be either of those two colors, too. Not red. Wing it with polar, not deerhair, so it will rapidly sink. Fish it on a floating line, but let it sink on a long leader as deep as it will go in medium-swift water. The strike can come anytime. Rear back as you would to any wet-fly take.

6. Fish the Bulkley Mouse, Moose Turd, and any Muddler Minnow as though it were a wet fly. Sink it deep. Fish it slowly, just off the bottom. Be prepared for the fly to stop, the line to continue to belly past the fish, and the increasing weight on the end of the line to indicate that you have a solid hook-up. Strike back decidedly and hard. Do it again. The fish ought to

move off with a rush.

The above ideas are put forward for discussion purposes mainly and to make the fisher think about what is involved in fly design and what (if anything) may be going through a steelhead's mind (such as it is) while it lies in a riffle, waiting for time to pass until a ripe female swims by.

If you get bored on a long eventless afternoon, put one or more of these exercises to work and see where they lead. There is a fairly good chance a steelhead will respond.

TWENTY-FOUR

The end of August can be an exciting time, for most of the summer steelhead will have already entered the North Fork and still be there, if there has not been rain enough to move them up into Deer Creek. There will also be salmon—Chinooks and, if it is an odd-numbered year, humpies. With the first of the salmon come Dolly Vardens, probably in search of the waste eggs from the salmon. They will spawn themselves later in fall in the headwaters.

Sea-run cutthroats are arriving daily, too. Possibly the salmon bring them in, with their eggs. Their spawning time is towards spring. All the while they are in the river they are avid feeders; the Dollies are also. Salmon are not, but they sometimes take wet flies, usually when they are newly arrived in a pool. Only very rarely will they take dry flies and when they do it is out of perversity and anger, for they cannot benefit from feeding and soon will spawn and die.

Walt Johnson reports taking a silver salmon on a dry fly. If anybody could do it, Walt could, and thirty years ago Dean Almvig told me about a humpy on a dry fly. I believe it. If a salmon will occasionally take a wet fly, it will take a dry fly, too, but only if the conditions are precisely right.

What conditions these are I have no idea, but I have my own theory. The water must be shallow and probably broken, with stones on the bottom. Certain conditions are requisite to bringing salmon there and having them take, either wet or dry. I believe that the faster the current and the shallower the water, and the more rippling, the better the chance is for a salmon to take a fly. Normally these fish lie in deeper water, where there is more cover and protection. Chinooks are famous for finding the deepest lies and remaining near the bottom until it is time to move onto the redds and spawn. They will budge for nothing, nobody.

One night late in August there were all kinds of adult salmonids in the river and I had been fishing hard for whatever would come to my fly. There were steelhead present, but they were potted and reluctant to take a fly. Dry was probably the best way of fishing now. There were so many humpies that—careful as you might be—you kept hooking them on a wet fly; then you either managed to let the hook slide off or you got a solid hook-up and had to play the fish long enough to know if it was not a steelhead before (1) breaking it off, (2) landing and releasing it.

Many of the humpies were foul hooked, but a number of them nailed the wet fly as it swept through the pool. I used to think it was mainly aggressive males that struck the fly, until I began hooking a disproportionate number of slim females. Finally I concluded the chance of hooking males or females had some relationship to how many of each sex were in the pool. Usually there were more males than females—like at a high-school dance. I decided the fish hit in equal numbers, based on their relative populations.

With the arrival of all the salmon, the steelhead had changed their river lies. The humpies had moved them off to the sides of the runs and out of the fast water they liked because of its high oxygen content and the protection it provided with its boulder bottom that made them invisible. Then the Chinooks—which were nearer to spawning than any of the other species—moved from the deepest water into a shallower run that was adjacent to their redds. This put them into the same water we were fishing for steelhead.

Meanwhile the Dollies and cutthroats roamed the slackened flows, Dollies preferring the swifter chutes and cutthroats the still water where we could often find them feeding. It was a ripe time to be out and the floating line was the perfect tool to avoid snagging salmon and to get the maximum action from any taking species.

I fished the Manure Spreader Hole, then walked down the long beach to the Elbow. I came back to the Spreader at near-dark and found Terry Blacker fishing it. He was a local friend.

Big dark fish occasionally rolled in the chop at the head of the hole. Naturally I started to fish there; I wanted my dry-fly water to be just as fast as this diminished river could provide. There were not many such spots left.

Fish splashed but did not strike. Many were humpy "splats"—a peculiar rise that looks much like a fish taking surface food and has caused trout fishers consternation, as they cover the rise, time after time, and nothing grabs their fly. Occasionally a Chinook stuck its broad back out of the riffle in what approximated a head-and-tail rise, but it was only nervous exercise. That back was black as coal.

I suspected that whatever steelhead remained in the North Fork had taken up unusual lies and were not easily moved. I had hopes for a cutthroat or two, or perhaps a Dolly; actually I would have been grateful for anything the river gave me. I was using six-pound test leader—a good indication that I still had dry-fly steelhead in mind. My fly was smaller than usual and dark, for darkness was down upon the river and it seemed appropriate. Terry stood downstream from me and I went in above him, as newcomers always do on my river and most others.

I threw the fly out into the chop and watched it ride a few inches before it disappeared in the gloom. A big back stuck itself out of the water and the head attached to the back ingested the fly. "Hey," I said softly to Terry. "Guess what?"

I was into a fish, but neither of us knew precisely what species. A big salmon then stuck its back out of the water. There was a fly in its mouth. Funny how you can see in low light a dark fly in the mouth of a black-mouthed salmon. It is mainly that something different is there, where it oughtn't be—a shape, a shadow, an outline.

"Is it a salmon?" Terry asked. "I think so." "You fishing wet?" he asked. "No, dry." "You're kidding?" "Yeah, that's how I feel about it, too. Big surprise."

There was not much action from the fish. It moved upstream about ten feet, slowly, then turned and ran straight down the center of the river for a little over thirty yards and stopped. Too slow for a steelhead, I decided. Too powerful, too.

Terry moved out of the water so I would have room to play the fish. Just then the fish ran across the river and jumped close to the far bank. We both saw it. "A Chinook," Terry said. "I'm sure it is a Chinook." "That's what I thought," I replied. "Isn't that something?"

It was indeed. I guessed the fish to weigh about sixteen pounds—a male. That is not awfully big for Chinooks. It is, in fact, about average. I began to play the fish carefully, which was not difficult, since the fish's moves were all slow and deliberate. A big, strong fish.

I said to Terry, "It just occurred to me that I may not land this beast. My leader is six pound and I think I've pulled about as hard as I dare." I tried to budge the fish, and he responded by moving a little. Snug up against the far bank, his head could be levered and I could persuade him to change his location by six or eight feet. But I could not get him to come any closer. And as soon as he had shifted once, he would move back to his former lie—and add another six feet or so to the distance between us. I was actually giving him line, grudgingly.

It dawned on me then—ten minutes into the battle—I would lose the fish for a variety of reasons, one of which was that it was growing dark fast. The fish jumped again (for the third time) and we could no longer see the fish itself only the bright edge of the splash. I became possessed with that desperation that comes when you know the odds are rapidly increasing against you. I began to pull harder, trying to persuade the fish to swim to me, where I could fight him on a shorter line. He wouldn't move. I tried "walking" him over, which is often a good trick and will move a steelhead when cranking won't work. The only result was a deeper bow in my rod.

I became concerned about the salmon's teeth; all that pulling might be raking the leader against those backward-slanting teeth of the black-jawed Chinook male. My feeling of futility mounted and it was a little like the onslaught of the flu.

"Terry, I don't know what to do. I think I'm going to break him off." He said nothing. I continued, "At least we both *saw* the fish. I mean, we know it to be a Chinook. And the Chinook *took* the dry. He wasn't foul-hooked. He was hooked in the mouth." "Right." "So I can break him, for I have nothing more to prove?" Silence. And break him I did.

I was instantly flooded with loss. How satisfying it would have been to have licked this great fish and seen the fly lodged in its jaw, the fish gasping in the shallows, but it was not to be. I've thought of asking Terry to sign an affidavit to testify that it was, certainly, a Chinook and, indeed, a dry fly and, indeed again, hooked fairly in the mouth, but fishers don't require this of each other, not the ones I know, anyway, and much time has passed and the whole ghostly evening seems a dream.

I know it happened, and will probably not happen again to me.

TWENTY-FIVE

The most adult salmonids I ever hooked and landed in a day was 13. It was an insane time and I shall never go through it again because I will quit long before that. Besides, I am older and have more sense, although friends will dispute this.

Mike Kinney

Again it was in August, some years back. It was again a time of low water, with a number of wild steelhead trapped in the runs below Deer Creek, a few Chinooks around, and humpies in abundance. The day was cloudy, which at this time of the year is greatly to the fisherman's benefit. It is when fishing dry fly is the most productive.

This is almost Mike Kinney's story, but not quite. Mike had borrowed a midge rod from Joe Monda, who had the cabin next door to his in the row of shacks behind the Oso General Store. It was a beauty and had been left to Joe when George Keough died.

The rod was an impregnated Orvis, about seven feet in length and (if I recall correctly) weighed just over two ounces. It had a tapered cigar grip and two rings of German silver over cork to form the reel seat.

To balance it and suitably keep it company was a Hardy Uniqua fly reel of about 3-1/8 inches in diameter. They had not been made for fifty years and were a precursor of the Perfect; they had a similar shape and an earlier pawl system, but lacked ball-bearings, a ring guide, and a ventilated spool.

On it was a weight-forward ivory dry line in a matched size, probably a five, since anything smaller wasn't made yet. It was a Scientific Angler Air Cel Supreme and George had gotten it gratis from Leon Martuch to use in the fly-casting classes he taught at Seattle University as one of the perks for teaching some education courses. He had given us his extra lines, which supposedly had small defects that kept them off the market; I could never find any in mine and, fifteen years later, it is still performing flawlessly, when other lines by other makers and SA have fallen apart.

George was always coming into good deals, which he kindly shared with us. Many of my reels and rods by Hardy and Orvis came into my hands via George, but not the midge rod nor the reel that went with it. They went to Joe. They were collectors' items and occasionally went at auction, the bidding reaching the stars. It was the kind of rare tackle obtainable only from a great friend's will. It is a sad way to get a treasured rod and reel, but it often happens.

Joe kindly lent the rod to Mike. Mike immediately became fond of the little wand and began to think of it as his own. It was the rod he often went out with on a warm evening to a river that had shrunk alarmingly, just as its fish population had expanded.

A cloudy day came along and Mike took the rod and reel down to the Spreader Hole for some morning exercise. He tied on a fly that looked much like a Gray Wulff and promptly caught two steelhead. He retired the fly to his cap, where ten years later it still jauntily rides. If you admire it, Mike will tell you the story without any prompting.

Frank Snyder also took a steelhead dry from the pool that morning. I arrived late and instantly regretted what I had missed. The action hadn't lasted long and was now over. I fished dry for the next hour and a half, working my way downstream, but without any success. I fished angrily, heatedly, not well, slamming out cast after cast and daring the steelhead to take my dry. Well, they wouldn't. So I switched to wet, and began catching fish. Most were humpies. The same conditions that made the steelhead take dry, at least for a while, made them and the salmon take wet all day long. I caught a salmon, a salmon, a salmon, a steelhead, a salmon, etc., throughout the long afternoon and into the evening. As dusk settled down on the Elbow, I found I had caught and released twelve fish, three of them steelhead. Of the humpies, most were fair-hooked. Oh, maybe three were not.

At dark I stood at the Manure Spreader Hole, where I had begun — where all of us had begun—that long-ago morning. I threw out cast after cast against the dying of the light. "One more fish," I prayed greedily. "I don't care what it is," but of course steelhead was on my mind.

The water was boiling with fish. Most were salmon. The Chinook tended to boom and fall back with a loud splash. The humpies jumped more like steelhead or else revealed themselves through their telltale splats.

My rod tip went down and a fish vaulted in the air. Oh, my aching back! I set the hook and played the fish. My reel ground out a complaint; I think it was dry as sand by now. I muscled the fish into shore and beached it, thrashing. It was a humpy, a slime creature, as ripe as they get—female, slender, pale green in the last glow, without discernible scales. George McLeod calls them "lizards with fins." I see the point, though I respect them because they are an essential part of river life, and thus are holy.

I nudged it back into the slack, reeled in, and headed home, disgusted with myself.

TWENTY-SIX

This year on the Wenatchee there was a good snowpack; there was, in fact, a good pack everywhere in the West. The North Fork stayed high well into August and when it finally dropped never reached the level of the recent drought years. The Wenatchee stayed high, too, until well into the season. It was a cool, wet year, and the river dropped slowly. Of course the diversion for irrigation purposes began to draw it down soon. I caught it very early, when it was at a height I knew was ideal and would not return to again until late fall, when the diversion ended, rains returned, and the river filled with water and with fish.

The late-summer volume was down to about 1400 cubic feet per second. At this height I knew I could wade the Camp Pool, though it would be challenging and exciting. Merlin's Pool would be too high to get out in even a few yards from the beach, which was a low bank. I would have to be content with the water around camp. The date was July 21, and I had never fished the Wenatchee before August 26, but decided to take a chance. The worst that could happen was another skunk in a lifetime of skunks from fishing for steelhead. Besides, it had rained hard on the west side and all our rivers were out. I had two day's vacation coming from working on my book and badly needed to be outside.

I arrived three hours before dark and set up my tent trailer. It was hot and by the time I had my shelter shipshape I was in a lather. What better way to cool down than to don waders and step deep into the cold river? I did, and promptly caught a steelhead, a big surprise.

It took only a short distance down the run. I was surrounded by running water thirty inches deep, with a cobbled bottom. It was not easy wading and a false step would send me stumbling and knock me down. Shore was a long ways off. Also, I had two dogs with me; I had Sam and I had my host Larry's dog, Tug—or I soon had her, two minutes after Sam announced the fish was on with his usual staccato barking. Tug knew just what he meant and joined us.

I thought the fish might be a Chinook, for I knew Chinook were already in the river and had seen one jump, but the fish immediately started doing steelhead things. It shook or rolled or whatever they do to produce that jagged effect on the line. Then the fish jumped and there was no doubt. It went for a long run and leaped again. All I could do was balance on my feet and watch it happen. Soon the fish was far downstream and across the river; as the spool on the reel ran freely. I followed the fish gingerly, picking my way, moving ever more slowly as the reel gave out line in a hurry.

The fish was into a tough spot. It was about a hundred and thirty yards out and far across the river. All the water was swift and no more than five feet deep. There was no quiet nook on my side into which to trick the fish and thrash it out. Every time I drew it in a little, it ran back out and, worse, across to the far side of the river again. Here the drift ended in a speedy tailout and a riffle that poured with a whitewater rush into the next pool, where I couldn't follow.

I fully expected to break off the fish and applied suitable pressure. I think that what happens in such an instance, if the leader doesn't break first, is that the fish *planes* across the river, either just under the surface or on it, for the shape of the fish, coupled to the hydrodynamic effect of the river, causes the fish to skate across the river to a position directly below you. This is not something the fish does willingly, mind you.

Soon the fish was directly below me, deep in the tailout but still decidedly above where the next pool begins. I slowly picked my way downstream through crotch-deep water and gathered line back onto my reel. Now the fish was fifty feet away, now thirty. I saw where my fly line changed color and that it was off the water. The splice came to the tip top, the fish less than twenty feet out.

Below me was a draw. Normally it was a slough; it contained a patch of slow water near a bank that was steep but normally wide and shallow enough to wade at wader-top height. Today it was a streamy patch lined with willow and young cottonwoods that were mostly underwater. It was the only place where I had a chance to beach my fish.

I had two dogs to contend with. Tug was a joy, a delight; she kept ever back and was intelligently watchful; she did not bark nor charge the fish and obeyed everything I told her to do, which wasn't much. It was only to stay behind me. Sam was the awful opposite.

I managed to lead the fish in and strand it on the willow-clad shingle where two seams of fast water came together and formed a pocket. I had to try three times before I made it, while backing up. Each time Sam went after the fish, in spite of my urging him not to. But when the fish was high and dry, he moved away, quick-eyed, eager for the release. I handled it as deftly as I could, under the circumstances. The fish was a female of about eight pounds; she had an adipose and a perfect dorsal. I did not think to take a picture or a few scale samples.

I stayed the night and fished the following morning. I touched nothing. It was way too early in the season to expect a fish and mine from yesterday was a fluke, but it indicated one thing—fish run in the Wenatchee throughout the year, though not many. It is a river that is hard to wade and to fish in more than a few places during high water; thus there is plenty of escapement. My plan was to fish it when the water height was exactly right for the Camp Pool and the wet fly would sink and swim the way I liked it to. I had watched the NOAA river gauge readings for a month, as the river slowly dropped. Since it worked once, I hope to return next year at the same height, regardless of the usual heat problem. (One-hundred degrees F. is not unusual in mid-summer.)

That is not how it turned out. I did not come back until September first. By then the river was dead low and my pool had formed its early backwater. I could see all the rocks on the bottom. The reading on the river gauge was 520 cfs. The river had shrunk to a third its former flow.

Dry line was the only way to fish to escape hanging up in the rocks and losing my fly. During the long afternoon the water was so warm that I parboiled in my plastic waders and Sam stood waded up to his chin, where he remained in spite of my urging him to go ashore.

I caught no fish but squawfish, a scrapfish that will hit a fly hard and sometimes save the day from being a complete loss. There is a $2 bounty on squawfish on certain reaches of the Columbia, but not here. They are a tough-looking, aggressive fish and belong to the river, though they eat scads of scrap fish and salmonid fry, which is why people hate them and there is a bounty.

Suckers could be seen along the seam of the pool, where the still water joins the flow that today was barely moving. They lay with their heads to the bottom, their bodies at about a thirty-degree angle, which explains how wet-fly fishermen snag them so often: the fly's path is where they offer the biggest target.

Watching the suckers vacuuming up the bottom, I realized what an important contribution they make to the health of the river. This caused me to reflect on the ugly scene of a few hours ago, on my way East. Three crows were hungrily disposing of what was left of a gray squirrel run over by a car. What made it ugly? The death of the squirrel? The squirrel fed the crows, without which such waste would remain indefinitely. We would have a lot of dead critters at roadside and elsewhere that would take forever to decompose without help.

Every so often I find a sucker or squawfish that some disdainful angler has caught and flung up high on the beach, thinking he is doing the river a favor. The fish rots and stinks. This is wrong. The fish belongs in the river. There when it dies it feeds the microscopic submarine world. Suckers perform much the same function the crows do with the squirrel.

At low water a river reveals itself nakedly. Also it heats up badly, often fatally, as fry and parr cook and die. Daytime temperatures surpass seventy degrees for short durations. Fortunately for the Wenatchee, the cooling mountains are not far away, and the early morning temperatures come back to the low 60s. Most fish adapt to the warm water successfully; some die. The fisher waits for the return of higher flows, lower temperatures, and the ascent of fresh steelhead from the deep reservoirs of the Columbia, where the water is often as much as fifteen degrees cooler.

I say to myself, "I should have stayed in the mountains and fished for trout," but, no, I must continue my pursuit of steelhead, bad times or not, high water or drought. A floating line and surface fly is the best way to fish the Wenatchee at such a slack time.

TWENTY-SEVEN

I pay close attention to the "seam." It is a good term, and I got it from Dec Hogan and Scott O'Donnell, two guides who use it to describe the place

The Camp Pool on the Wenatchee.

where fast water and slow come together. In some runs, it is clearly observed, but in others it may be more difficult to locate, for the river is running all over the place and only seems to shallow and deepen and lose its slick surface quality but slightly; this is the place to fish. Learn to recognize it. The seam is where steelhead love to hang out and it is where experienced steelheaders look to find them, year after year, in water new or old to them.

As the river drops, the seam moves—generally out towards the center of the river. The area in which steelhead lie shrinks and the fish become concentrated. This is one reason why dry-fly fishers wait until most of the snow runoff is gone before they stop wet-fly fishing in spring: the fish are too spread out in a wide river and the wet fly is more efficient in presenting itself to them over a longer drift. As the fish become centered along the seam, or in other good lie spots with a broken bottom, where swift water and slow come together, the river seems to deepen, and boulders appear; the dry-fly fisher can direct his attention to fewer locations and have a much better chance of raising a fish.

There is one exception to the seam rule. It is the tailout of a pool, where the water quickens and no discernible seam is to be found, the river fanning out and running at a uniform speed and deepening only slightly along the far bank. It is excellent water to fish, wet or dry.

A typical pool will have a general vee-like configuration, whatever its height. Steelhead like water to be running at a good speed—quick, but not too quick, over a bouldery bottom. They will always seek it out and, thus, certain pools on some rivers will always hold fish in about the same places, when at the same height. This changes only when the pool is drastically altered, say as the result of flood or other disaster.

Picture the vee-shaped pool, or rather a long pool with the current forming a vee and the narrowest point of the vee to your left. (The river flows to your right.) In other words, the vee is tipped on its side and turned clockwise ninety degrees. When the water is high in spring, the vee expands and seemingly loses its shape, filling the river from bank to bank. But along the edge with the bar (although the bar may be underwater at this time), the water slows and shallows. This is where the fish will be lying. They will be shunning the strongest current and seeking the same-speed water they will be lying in even when the river drops.

Nearly always they choose to rest where there is water of this favorite speed. In high water the angler will fish the edges of the river, almost always the near edge—the edge with the bar under it. And it is just as well, for with a river so high he cannot wade very far out nor be able to cast but a fraction of its width. If he tries to fish water that is too fast, his line will be whipped downstream—since it most likely is a sinking line now, it will not have time to descend and fish, for even the highest density lines require some slowness in order to descend.

The seam, such as it is, lies near the shore, though it may be hard to see and have fewer seam-like characteristics than it will have once the river drops.

As the river moves in the direction of mid-height, the wading bar appears and the angler can gingerly poke out into the swift current and cast to the seam. The slow water will still be running fast, but not so swiftly where he is standing, so a seam of sorts is beginning to form. The angler should recognize it for what it is and concentrate his attention there; it is still wet-fly time. Now his line will sink, but to get near bottom it needs to be a line of considerable density. Fish should be running the river and the angler who allows his fly to sweep the water on his side, as he moves slowly downstream, should be hooking the occasional fish. He may hook one only after much wading and casting and seemingly at random, because they are not concentrated yet and may lie in many locations. He is depending on luck for his fly to pass in front of a resting steelhead that is one of many rapidly ascending the river now.

The river drops more. Good. The fisher wades deeper, the seam becomes more apparent (he says, "How did I ever miss it earlier?"), and the fish begin to concentrate. The water is warming, as is the air. The fingerlings that are left in the river begin to feed and sometimes dimple the surface. The fresh steelhead that have run into the pool occasionally rise or roll now, giving their presence away. They are not feeding—cannot utilize food successfully—but all the elements are right for them to come to the surface and take a fly.

There are several theories about this, and they all sound similar. Haig-Brown calls it "river memory." It means the fish revert back to their days as fry and parr, when they had to gobble river food in order to grow big enough to smolt and leave the river for that wider pasture, the sea. He says it is when the water temperature first reaches 55 degrees F. They are inclined to become trout-like then.

It is also the time when the river starts to shrink and the seam to grow evident.

Lee Wulff says much the same thing, but calls the action a "conditioned reflex." River conditions cause them to behave as they did as juvenile steelhead, they know not why. He says it is because they are bored. (This gives us something in common.) Bored, they are looking for "action." They grow restless, nervous. They feel the need to reassure themselves with proof of their strength and speed, and they will strike something new or challenging that enters their environment.

Wulff locates his fish and presents them with a wide range of fly patterns and sizes, trying to goad them into striking. It has no relationship to feeding, he says. He will spend hours, if necessary, trying to seduce a spotted fish. And often the fish he has made nervous reveals its restlessness by shifting its position near the bottom and "flashing."

Lee writes, in an article "How to Use Dry Flies for Atlantic Salmon": "The trout angler looks only for rises that actually show a fish breaking the surface; the salmon angler must look for flashes of the fish well down in the water. Failure to spot these interested fish, whose presence may be given away only by the slightest flash or shadowy movement, often means the difference between success and failure. For of a dozen salmon in a pool, many of which may be porpoising and leaping, the one most likely to take the fly is the one that shows restlessness when it passes over him."

Lee goes on, "A salmon may rise only a foot from the bottom and still be two or three feet under the fly on his first show of interest, but if the angler sees him, he has found a likely prospect and is on his way to some sport." [Page 41, *Fishing With Lee Wulff,* Knopf, 1972.]

Ah, finally. Somebody else has seen the flash. I am not alone or mad. In my book *Steelhead Water* I mentioned seeing a flash several times deep in the run directly under my fly, a flash that was too long to be a parr or whitefish and too silvery to be a sucker or darkening salmon. On my next cast the steelhead usually took the fly. I hooked the fish and, most of the time, landed it. It didn't happen often, but enough to be notable.

When I asked Walt Johnson about the flash before the rise, and if he had experienced it, he said, "No." I decided my experience was odd, atypical. Now Lee confirms it—but with Atlantic salmon. Well, many of us believe that the two fish have great similarities. Our fly fishing for steelhead owes a heavy debt to salmon literature and to the techniques described therein, but there has always been a point of departure. I'm not so sure there is one now.

The flashes I've seen have always been along the seam in a river shrunken to its summer low, and this is how I—a poor spotter of fish—managed to observe it. It took no skill or keen vision. It would have been hard to miss, as a matter of fact. The seam at such a time is pretty close to the strongest current the river has to offer. It contains the ideal speed the steelhead is seeking. In fact, it is the only water around that meets the fish's criterion.

Wulff says that since the salmon (or steelhead) has no hunger (as does a trout) for you to appeal to, you must work on its "mind."

Wulff is not humorless, but when he mentions the steelhead's mind I detect no evidence of irony or wit. He is speaking dead seriously. The angler must play "mind games" with his fish, he is implying. This is not so strange on both their parts as it might seem. Wulff likens the salmon's take of a surface fly that can give it no nourishment, no sustenance, to a young boy going out of his way to kick a tin can. Exactly.

It is perverse, ornery; boredom and ennui motivate it. It brings up matters of existence and essence. And there is an element of Zen Buddhism in the weirdness of the situation.

Steelhead lie in water of a certain speed and search until they find it. They also seek cover, protection, and security. Some pools offer practically no shade, but steelhead still hold in them; they must have other compensating characteristics, such as boulders, current, and depth. Conversely, if the river offers shade, the bottom need not be so boulder-strewn, nor so deep, nor so fast. This makes sense. A fish is always alert to the avenues of escape. If you wade out toward him, he may not shoot away, not if an avenue is open to him and he knows he can avail himself of it at any moment.

Skindivers report that steelhead back down a pool until they come to the tailout, where they attempt to hold. As the swimmers come near them, the fish do not slide over the end of the pool and into the chute at the start of the next run that would shelter them. Instead, they shoot up *past* the swimmers, fleeing at top speed upstream, and take up protected lies there.

This is identical to what a hooked fish does. The steelhead goes into its flight behavior, we might call it. It does not vary much from fish to fish or pool to pool. A hooked steelhead will do everything he can to rid himself of the hook—run, jump, roll. But he will not leave the pool, not unless he can't help it. A fisher can capitalize on this and save himself a lot of trouble. Stories of fish that have left their pools and taken the angler far downstream usually indicate a fish poorly played. The fish will circle down the pool, or run through it, but he will almost always stop low in the tailout and hold there. He wants to remain in the pool. I want him to, too.

If I pull too hard at this time, or if my fish gets too tired and is washed into the tailout, where the current is swiftest, he may spill over into the next pool. The trick is to manage him so that this doesn't happen. It's not as hard as it sounds. One good way is not to crank your fish up from the tailout, but to walk him up. Clamp down on the reel or line and start walking backwards. Chances are good the fish will follow you upstream. If a lot of line is out, you may have to walk back downstream, retracing your route and continuing to reel in slack at the same rate as you are walking, in order to tow your fish back upstream again and gain the rest of the line.

Note: it usually won't work if you try to crank him. He will only tow. Of course you will have to crank in the slack you've gathered. This is okay and works well. Very few fish will crank upstream against their will, against the current. You have to know which to try, from trial and error, and treat each fish accordingly.

The worst thing that can happen is, late in the fight, a tired fish slips into the tailout and is too tired to swim back up; the current carries him over the lip and into the next pool. Then you must scramble after him, and often the river changes banks here and you arrive on the deep side, where the trees grow down to the edge and you cannot follow him. Almost always you lose the fish. It is your fault, but nobody will challenge you if you blame it on the river.

It is fun and instructive to spot fish lying in the river and try to approach them. A located fish that will let you come near without flight is aware of your presence but may feel no threat, not until you do the wrong thing. Wiping your nose with the back of your hand can do it. (It will also send treed birds flying, I've found.) It is not the time to reach for your fly box, either. Yet situations vary. A fish that has been disturbed may quickly regain its calm and become susceptible to a fly properly presented. This may be because the flight mechanism occurs may times in the day and is not serious in itself, only vaguely alarming in nature; that is, the fish does not feel threatened. It is simply triggered to react and the action is to move away from the threat. (I cannot exactly imagine a steelhead being "afraid.")

All these ideas and notions are the result of many thoughts and theories that come to a reflective angler during the course of a day. He must "step into the mind" of the salmon or steelhead, as Wulff tells us to do with a straight face. The fish is not motivated as a trout is by "thoughts" of food. Food is useless to the steelhead or Atlantic salmon. (Wulff likens the situation to an adult man trying to sustain himself on a diet of two or three blueberries.) The fish's sense of boredom and aggression is triggered by the right approach. In low water the surface fly is most apt to be it.

TWENTY-EIGHT

The vee narrows as the river drops and the water off to the side of the channel becomes slack. The seam is evident. On the bank side the river forms little pockets against the rocks where there is no current. A fly will hang there until the belly of line in what is left of the current whips it away. For practical purposes the bank pockets don't fish well with the fly and are not good places to try to catch a steelhead.

Similarly, on your side, the formerly straight shot of strong current that carried your wet fly smoothly through the pool and, later, your dry, has now developed a terrible back eddy; you've seen it coming and dreaded its arrival. It causes your fly to . . . die. It becomes a lifeless, inert object, and it is the moving fly that attracts the taking steelhead in a pool.

Another way of putting this is that your chances of getting a fish to hit are greatly decreased because of the river's slack and slowness.

The classic way of fishing such water is illustrated in Jock Scott's book about A.H.E. Wood, *Greased Line Fishing for Salmon [and Steelhead]*, cited earlier. (Jock Scott is a phony name, drawn from the literature of fly tying; the man's real name is Donald G. Ferris Rudd.)

In Figure 14 of his book, the pocket or slack water lies behind a rock,

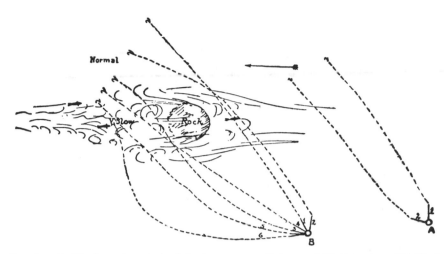

Shows how the difficult area beyond a band of quiet water can easily be covered. B1. Cast and mend B2. Mend again from 3 to 4. Allow fly to be drawn gently from 5 to 6 by letting the rod swing round. Compare the diagram with Figure 15.

and Scott (or Rudd) tells us we are to cast pretty much directly cross-stream and make the first upstream mend immediately. A moment later, we make the second, also in the same direction and without moving the fly. The fly is allowed to sink by giving it slack and by moving the belly above it twice. The third mend is made and it is downstream; this "leads" the fly into the dead water and actually (or so our experience tells us) pulls it around in the water, speeding up its course and making it seem less lifeless.

The illustration—also accompanied by one from a vertical perspective, showing the sunken boulder and the swirl of current and the slack behind the boulder (Figure 15)—has always bothered me.

If I were to fish a pool exactly like this one, with a slow flow running down it and a boulder in the same place, my fly would not behave this way. It would hang, then whip. It would not sink very much and do most of whatever it is doing near the surface. Because of the backwater, the fly wouldn't come anywhere near the taking plane of the two fish pictured as lying almost on the bottom, just behind the boulder. It would miss them by a mile and they would have no inclination to chase after it, not if I know steelhead.

I would rather try for the two fish lying above the rock, especially the one with the station near the top. This appears to be a taking fish, and if I stand above him and rest him after I have waded into my casting position I am fairly confident he will take my *waking* fly on the first cast. If not, the

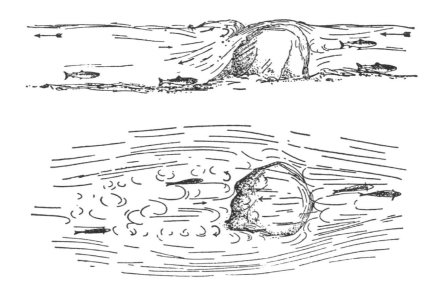

These show the way in which a fly can be sucked down behind a stone.

second fish that lies deeper above the rock may do so.

Of the four fish, the lower two are adjudged non-takers, the one higher in the water column a probable, and the one above that which is nearer the bottom a maybe. One taking fish out of four is a good average. It requires only a few such situations to make true that axiom, "Have a nice day."

Another one of Scott's illustrations a few pages earlier also bothers me, for it is contrary to my experience. (Scott's Figure 6.) Yet it has its value. This one shows a salmon missing a fly twice on the same drift and taking it the third time. The caption reads: "A fish has missed the fly at A, has swam round to take it at B, has again missed it, and only succeeded it taking in properly at D." (C is the line position for the take at D and E is where the fish moves off to from D, heading upstream and drawing the fly into the hinge of its jaw because of the belly that has formed.)

What I don't like about the illustration and caption is that the salmon (or steelhead) has "missed" twice. I don't believe that they miss at all. I believe that they hit what they strike, but they may rise "falsely" to the fly and not open their mouth to take it. It is hard to see and, once seen, even harder to believe. A steelhead or Atlantic salmon may come numerous times to a fly, bunting it, pushing a wave in front of it that moves it away, or even come crashing down on it. In none of these instances is the fish taking the fly; neither is it "missing" it. Often its mouth is closed.

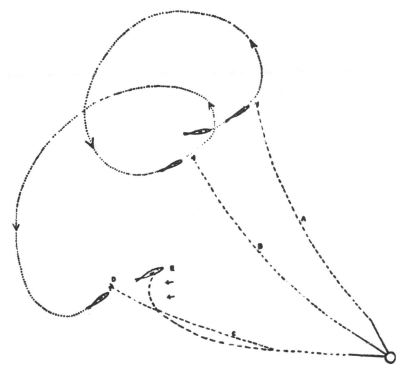

A fish has missed the fly at A, has swum round to take it at B, has again missed it, and only succeeded in taking properly at D.

Alec Jackson tells me he has had a fish take at the same place in three consecutive casts. Come to think about it, so have I. He feels that when the fish "misses" or rejects the fly, the fault is his. He asks himself, "What did I do wrong?"

I don't do this. I am quick to pat myself on the back for having done something right, though of course I have no hook-up to show for it. I blame the steelhead. After all, many times I get a solid strike on a sloppy cast or one following a terrible presentation.

A good book that pursues the problem of a dragging fly attracting or not attracting fish is Jock Scott's *Fishing Fine and Far Off, Salmon Fishing in Practice,* c. 1952. It is a superior book and contains 52 pages on controlled drag alone. Scott maintains that drag is impossible to avoid and Wood wasn't saying that you could, only that you should fish with as little of it as possible. In other words, it should be managed and manipulated to the angler's advantage. In a few cases, it can be reduced to next to nothing, but always there is the line and leader attached to the fly, and they are pulling on it. It is better to recognize it and take it into consideration, making it work for you, rather than the other way round.

The problem is also addressed in Frederick Hill's *Salmon Fishing, The Greased Line On Dee, Don and Earn,* 1948. Hill, a ghillie on the Dee and other rivers, knew Wood well and believed that the Dee was exceptional. The Carlogie beat, for instance, which Hill fished for twenty years, is near the Cairnton water, but fishes much differently. Hill addressed it with a dragging fly, one carefully controlled for the most part as Scott said worked well on every other river and every other beat on the Dee but Wood's. So we must temper our reading with experience and trust what it tells us.

The fish may be following the fly, almost taking it, bulging it, or even bunting it, but not taking it; that is, accepting it in its mouth. It is theoretically possible the fish decides to take on the third such pass at it, but I have my reservations. The fish either takes or it doesn't.

What I like about the illustration is that it shows a fish moving in a flow of water that has a current running down its middle. The circular movement the fish makes coming to the fly is, I believe, what truly happens whenever we get a rise or a take. The second circle of the fish to the fly is probably how the fish would behave on a second inspection, for the fish must ever keep its snout pointed upstream. (This is the same reason a fish can't run downstream forever; it must eventually stop and face upstream in order to work its gills—its equivalent of breathing. It is important to remember when you hook a great fish and it heads for the sea: soon it is going to have to stop and face the current again.)

The illustration is also good because it shows excellently how a fish gets hooked. No matter how much the line is mended, a big belly forms. The belly is essential to casting, though a big nuisance to fishing afterwards. It is the belly—dry line or wet—that continues on its course when the taking fish halts the fly in its tracks, which is always downstream and back towards the angler.

The belly, aided by the strike, is what hooks the fish. Often with a small sharp hook, the belly alone does the job. The strike is redundant. It is unnecessary and extreme. Yet I always strike my fish, given the chance. When the hook catches in the hinge of the jaw and the belly draws it home, the angler's strike merely results in jerking the fish's head around. When he strikes a second and a third time, the fish's head is snapped round again and again. This is probably deeply satisfying to the angler, but results in goading the fish into a long run which will hurry along its tiring and lead it more quickly to the beach.

Knowing this little, I will probably continue foolishly striking my fish repeatedly, for I do not want to leave anything to chance. If my hook is as sharp as I think it is, this will ensure it being firmly seated—if not in the hinge (which requires little or no action on my part), then in some tougher, more resistant part of the fish's mouth. I do this from habit. Every fish I've landed I've struck—and I've struck many a fish I haven't landed, it only follows. I should guess that about half of these fish would have been landed without the strike.

That is too low a percentage to bank on.

TWENTY-NINE

Soon the vee marking the seam becomes a wrinkle, the current all but gone and a huge backwater looms on the fisher's side. How does he proceed, now that the river has become a lake and he can see the top of every rock in the river? As best he can, for fly fishing is a pragmatic sport, and all the theory and illustrations accompanying the theories go out the window when you step into the water. Then it is just you and your river.

I would suggest the trout fisher's maxim: casting fine and far off. Stick to the floating line of your choice and throw it far downstream. Go down to six- or four-pound test leader and the smallest flies. Try trout patterns. Fish in the morning and the evening. Take long breaks. Read a book and wait for the irrigation diversion to end, the rains to come, the nights to get cold, the fish to arrive. For in such a warm, still river there are not apt to be many steelhead, and those few will be finicky. Still, it is fun to try to get one to hit and see what it looks like—when and if you get it to the beach.

Steelhead lie wherever they used to—along the seam, near boulders, in the deepest water, in runs with the strongest current and the most oxygen. Funny, but trout fishers seek the same water. Well, almost.

There is a man who chain-smokes on the North Fork, wears hip boots, and professes to catch large numbers of "trout." I've watched him closely. In spite of the shrunken river, we never seem to be fishing the same type of water. "Every hook a steelhead while you're trout fishing?" I asked him. His answer was evasive and all-knowing. He gets great joy out of hooking one-year-old steelhead—parr of about five or six inches. And I'm sure he catches his fair share of sea-run cutthroats in the fall. But he never hooks a steelhead, he says. Nor does he wish to.

He is fishing the wrong kind of water, or, from his perspective, it is the right water. He wants trout. The fact that he hooks and kills inadvertently a high percentage of next year's steelhead smolts doesn't bother him. Actually, he is proud of his skill in doing so. I've seen him beam when another five-incher hits hard and is brought thrashing to the hand for release. I dislike him immensely, for he is an adult and should know better; long ago, he should have put aside this childish endeavor and taken up an adult pastime. This is, after all, a steelhead river.

I am sometimes concerned that I do not hook many "trout," or steelhead juveniles. Perhaps I am fishing "wrong," even when fishing dry. That's all right with me.

I respect a good trout fly fisher. He knows a lot and practices more daily talent and skill and critical fly selection than I ever do. What he does is far more difficult than what I attempt, and if we go "fish for fish," his catch numbers much more than mine, every day. (I think I have him beat in sheer poundage, though.) When I say that, in my old age, I'd like to become a really good trout fisher (and live in Montana), I'm not being insincere or facetious. I mean it, at least for the moment, for the steelheading is slow.

Thirty

The pears are all picked, the golden delicious apples have acquired their blush and the reds are thick and lush upon the bough, red as an October sky. I know the goldens must be picked first and the reds held to the tree with chemicals sprayed from the air before they will grow ripe enough for harvesting. That time is a few weeks off. With it comes the bulk of the Wenatchee's run of steelhead. Meanwhile a few of the Main Line diversions have kicked in and there has been rain in the mountains, though none here, and the river has risen a few inches, raising the cfs to around 700. It's not what I want, but it's what I'll take, and be grateful for, and enough to start me fishing again in earnest.

The back eddies have disappeared from most good pools, and a floating line will stay taut during its ride down the center; you still have to mend, but now your mends don't come drifting back at you with a big, unavoidable belly that you are unable to cope with. Your fly rides out its course nicely, the line trailing behind it, the mends meaningful and purposeful. And a few fresh fish have trickled into the river.

The water in the morning is in the low 60s still and warms up to near 70 during the long, sun-ridden afternoons. If you want to bathe in the river, it is pleasant and there is no shock. The soap washes right off, as in the shower, so after a hot afternoon's fishing, you walk right into the Camp Pool in your skivvies, lather up, scrub your head, and splash off all the suds of your biodegradable, non-foaming soap. You towel down and sit in an aluminum lawn chair in what's left of the day, letting the sun bake your hair. It takes just over an hour to dry and then you are ready for dinner.

There is an hour left in which to fish and you decide on a short drive to Merlin's Pool, hoping to find it unoccupied but deciding already ahead of time that if there is only one angler you will join him. If there are two, and they have craftily divvied up the water between them so there is no room for a third, you will go on to one of the Monitor Bridges and give the riffles there a quick go-through.

But Merlin's is empty.

You and your dog walk in rapidly through the orchard, the goldens to the right, the reds to the left. The goldens are beginning to fall of their own weight and orchardist Ken has his bins in place. Picking will start in a day or two. You mark by eye a few newly fallen apples and plan to pick them up (if they don't have mouse bites or brown spoilage spots already) on your way out. They'll need a week or so to ripen and add to their sugar content, if this year is like any other, but you always eat at least one tart, and shudder, but have no stomach ache to show for it, which you now believe is a folktale told to young boys to keep them out of orchards. Already you can taste in the back of your mind the crisp bite of a golden and its pungent clasp upon your tongue, and know that it is good. But fishing is on your mind, not apples.

You find the rise in the river not really discernible and are a little disappointed. The worse thing you can imagine for this pool is too high water, which keeps you along the shore, where there is no room for a backcast and you are able only to cover a pathetic one-tenth of the necessary distance to reach the nearest lie where a fish might be resting.

Today you can walk right up to that place and past it. You enter higher in the pool than you wish because you know from the past that it will sometimes give you a quick fish, even though the Great Flood of 1990 destroyed much of the top substrate and you will be fishing through about eighteen inches of water until you have shuffled downstream and come to the slick caused by the second submerged boulder on your side of the river, where the true start of the pool now lies.

With a sinking line the boulder is a hazard. A floating line, however, is up to the challenge, and you immediately throw out a long cast tight to the bank, make one mend, and let the surface fly drag fetchingly across in a narrow, downstream arc. In the past, you've had fish come rushing up to seize it in just this location, throwing spray and porpoising several times thrillingly. Today, nothing happens.

Without moving your feet you make a second cast to exactly the same spot, mend, strip off another five feet of line, and mend again, allowing the fly to drift a couple of yards farther without drag before it begins its taut swing and artificial wake. Again there is no pull.

You move downstream with a shuffling side step, for it is difficult wading here, as well as throughout this pool, and though you know it as well as anybody, you suppose, you are always making some small error where the pool deepens and slows, and almost plunge in over your wader tops. Or else you go stumbling over some ledge and do a little dance on your toes before regaining your balance. Always on the verge of falling in, you realize that you never have, not once in this difficult pool, and the news brings an assurance that is misleading.

Your fly is a buggy little no-name thing, scruffy, dark. It came off your fly tying vice looking only half as good as you intended it. Its appearance is better than you deserve; the fly is a happy error, and ever since you touched varnish to its head you have been dying to fish it, it looks so grubby and natural. What fish can resist it? Well, all the fish so far today.

Several times you have stripped it back in and let it dangle in the current out from you, rolling the line back and forth until you are able to watch it sweep by in the shallows. Wow. It looks like every good, edible thing in the river—sculpin, caddis larva, salmon fry, stonefly. So far today you have only hooked one squawfish and two juvenile steelhead on it. Still, you have a good feeling about it and know it will produce, given half a chance. How much time is "half a chance?" Till dark, you decide.

You come to the cement slab and your pulse quickens. You have had many strikes at the top of this pool, but you have had most a third of the way through it. Two-thirds of the way through it is nearly as good, and down at the bottom, where the current seems to disappear (but really doesn't), the water is good, too. In fact, the whole pool is uniformly excellent throughout its length, which doesn't mean that at special times certain parts of it aren't better than others.

Today you expect a fish in the top third. You expect it so confidently that you have moved systematically through the section and out of it before you realize you haven't touched a steelhead, though your fingertips and wrists (and I suppose your nose and toes) are ready for one. You come to the lonely pine (the Lonely Pine Motel, you think: everybody welcome), but linger above it. This is the true heart of this pool and it is where everybody slows down annoyingly —annoyingly, that is, if you are in a lineup above this fisher. You can't help yourself, nor can he, for the water is so lovely, with its deep boulders and ledges and bubbly rip along the surface. From your memory rise up images of fish you'd thought you'd forgotten, and you see them leap anew into the camera of your mind, silhouetted against the very river you are now staring at, in which nothing at all is happening.

Nothing if you don't count the great blue heron soaring overhead, wings extended in a long, sloping glide, trailing its shadow that grown men have been known to cringe at as it passes over them from behind. Nothing, too, if you don't pay attention to the paired dippers flying in flashy formation and performing acrobatics that no birds truly can, only jet aircraft. Nothing if you don't include the merganser brood playing the ducky equivalent of kick-the-can at the tail of the pool, a hundred and forty yards away by rough count.

A mink scurries along the bank opposite, dodging in and out of the rocks, playing hide-and-go-seek with itself or its ghostly shadow. It is a Zen experience—well, a little like one—for first you see it, then you don't. Is there really a mink? You bet you. Where is it? Well, you can't see it. Then there isn't any mink. Look—there it goes. Where? Didn't you see it? No. Then I guess there isn't a mink.

A man from a car parked on the shoulder comes down the steep bank in tennis shoes, carrying a spin rod and tackle box. He moves to a point exactly opposite you. (Thanks a lot. Why do they always do this, when there is a half-mile of open water above and below where you are fishing?) He heaves a spoon into your water and your heart sinks; you know if you fished spoons in such a run, and did it right, you would hook umpteen steelhead. The trick is in doing it right, and you aren't going to bother relearning old tricks at this stage in your advancing senility.

The man reels in slowly and your heart turns in your chest with each spin of his handle. Now . . . now—you expect the strike. Nothing. You have briefly forgotten your own fishing. The man casts again, waits a moment longer, and begins to reel in just as slowly. He hooks a rock and the rod bows from the weight, not a fish. For a moment there. . .

The man whips his line back and forth through the water and the air. He has a good hookup. Finally—angry—he pulls too hard and breaks off. Serves him right for crowding you. You make a cast while he ties on another spoon—how many does he have in the tackle box, you wonder? A dozen? You remember that, in this pool a man often stays until he has lost an average of 3.4 spoons or Mepps spinners. In some cases, this takes him about ten casts. In other cases, 3.4 lures will last a man up to twenty minutes.

Zip goes spoon number two. Gad, how far and how easily a spinning reel casts a medium weight. It isn't inefficient and muscular, like fly fishing. Nor is it as much fun. You watch intently and your body bends in empathy to the man's crank of the reel, as you picture a steelhead peeling out of formation and nailing the flashing wedge of metal. No strike again. Why doesn't the man move on and try the water just a few yards downstream, stepping along like we fly fishers do, always presenting our humble fly to new fish in different lies? Why do they stand ever in one place? Do they expect the fish to come to them? Is this why they catch fewer fish than they should, considering the efficiency of the tackle and the handful of steelhead you know to be in the pool?

You keep moving along, but he stays in the one place, thankfully. It is where you were when he first spotted you. ("Got your place," he must be thinking. "Nyah, nyah.") You continue to cast, drift, and retrieve. Step down and repeat the process. Soon you are at the culvert. Your colleague (who did not reply when you said howdy) continues to cast into the same drink and has lost his second spoon.

What do they cost, you wonder? Buck, buck and a half? Two? It's been a couple of decades since you bought a spoon. You must be getting old, when you think of your fishing in terms of ten-year spans and half your friends are no longer fishing because they're dead.

The man strikes again and his rod bows. Damn, a fish, you think. But it is another rock. The rock is determined, resolute. The rock defeats the spoon and the line to which it is attached. Three, you count. A prudent gear-fisher would leave now, in financial defeat: the bank broke him. You see him standing there, the limp nylon dangling from his rodtip. He is deliberating. Risk one more rig or leave? Your body torques to help him with the decision. Leave, your shoulders urge.

Your brain waves convince him. Leave he does. You can't believe your great luck. This is nearly as good as a fish. You sag in your boots in relief.

Opposite the culvert the river begins to widen largely. It seems to double its depth and width every fifty feet. A slight upstream wind has picked up, but it is nothing like it gets, say, around eleven o'clock in the morning. That is the time, you remember, Ernest Hemingway told the wind to ever come alive.

An upstream wind to a right-hander fishing from the right bank of a river tends to blow the line and fly into his face. To keep this from happening, he hurries his backcast. If you hurry your backcast, you shorten the line-loading capability of the rod and are able to cast less far. To cast as far as you want and need to, you begin to exert more muscle on your forward cast that follows the foreshortened backcast. The line goes less far. You are getting tired, your muscles sore.

Because of the breeze—we don't call this wind; wind is what will come up Hemingwayesquely late tomorrow morning—you tip your rod tip outward a few more degrees. This decreases the power in your forward stroke, though you haven't quite figured it out yet. You only know you are casting about fifty-five feet, where you were casting seventy or seventy-five before. What's more, you have waded even deeper, trying to move closer to the far shore that is ever receding; this effectively shortens the distance your line will travel through the air before it strikes the water behind you. To compensate for this factor, you put even more muscle into your casting than before. Still it slaps the water behind you. Surprise: you are casting an even shorter distance and now your bad shoulder begins to ache. Soon it will be dark and you can go home. Boy, fishing is sure a lot of fun. Especially fly fishing.

About this time the steelhead (who is about as bored as you are) decides to take your fly. "Why not?" he asks himself, for he has nothing else to do to occupy what Lee Wulff humorlessly calls his "mind."

The steelhead swings in behind the fly that is behaving most unnaturally, following around through the water this huge belly of thick floating line. The leader that attaches the fly to the fat yellow line is visible throughout its length and casts a shadow-like clothesline on the sand. The fly *dangles* from the leader in an inert and unattractive position.

Evidently this is just what the steelhead wants today. And—lucky for you—it sometimes happens. (I know, I know: similarly meteors penetrate the atmosphere, but this happens about as often, for reasons just as inexplicable.)

The steelhead swims over to where the hapless fly hangs in what's left of the current and sucks it in. It does so in a dainty fashion, for no clear reason. As Lee Wulff puts it, it is the equivalent of a man starving in a forest eating one blueberry. Once in its mouth, the steelhead turns and returns to its lair. As it does so, it becomes aware of something trailing after it. The thing has no weight, not at first, and the steelhead is not alarmed, but the weight or pressure is building, and about the time the fish gets to its lie, it becomes alarmed. This is exactly the same moment that you realize something unusual has happened to your fly. It has acquired . . . substance. It is as though you caught some river weed and the fly is trailing it. Lift the rod to free the fly from the weed. That's it.

The fish, thoroughly alarmed, does its steelhead "thing." It takes off. It jumps. It shakes its head. It decides to return to the Columbia, where life is gentler and kinder and less unusual.

The hills of Monitor are lavender now, the setting sun squat behind them. There is an olive glow in the air, along with the russet scent of apples.

Your fish is an active presence in a river that would be sparkling and wonderful, even without steelhead, but with steelhead in it is simply marvelous. You experience epiphany.

Nobody should come between a man and his epiphany, not even a fellow fisher. Surely not a fishing writer. Me, I think I will sneak off and have me another green apple, tart as early sin.

THIRTY-ONE

Picture this: The fly you put in front of a steelhead may represent its first encounter with man, if it is wild. (If not, it will have had numerous previous encounters and probably have been handled several times.) The fish is three or four years old and has lived, first, in the river, then in the encompassing sea, traveling the vast Pacific as far as the coast of Asia to find the forage fish on which it and its school has fed like hogs in order to grow strong and big. In order to return to this self-same river in which to spawn and most likely die.

It has passed several huge, river-spanning dams on the Columbia successfully (both as smolt and as returning adult), come to the mouth of the Wenatchee, turned left, swam under the highway bridge, under the railroad trestle, the aqueduct, moved from riffle to pool to riffle to pool, and finally arrived at the resting spot you have carefully worked your way down to, while casting a floating line and fly repeatedly. The fish (whatever its reasons, and books have been written about this, to no firm conclusion) takes your fly. You hook and play and release it.

This is its sole contact with the world of people. Afterwards it lives on. It spawns and in the Columbia system dies. Its progeny continue its life. Isn't it simply wonderful? Aren't you the lucky one? I have never stopped believing this. And caught on a fly, too. Why on earth would it take a *fly*? Rather, why in water would it?

Some uninformed people believe that fly fishing is sporting. It is some sort of handicap with which we equip ourselves to go out and catch a fish in spite of ourselves and our equipment. It is to laugh.

Fly fishing on a low summer river, or one running at mid-height and turning cold, is the deadliest way of fishing. It is no handicap. It is just the opposite.

The good fishing for wild steelhead on the Grande Ronde River happened not so long ago that there are not people alive who remember when it was "discovered," that is, popularized beyond the acknowledgement of the locals, who were all meat fishermen and used gear.

When the water was low, and the fish were running, the gear fishers (then as now) did not do well. It was not until the fly fishers arrived that incredible numbers of steelhead started being caught, many by a single man in one day.

The locals liked this not at all. They became sullen and resentful. Worse, they became mean. They did unfriendly things like letting the air out of your tires and throwing barbed wire into a hole fly fishers liked. The idea was, the fisher's gear was supposed to hang up on the coiled wire, but since the flies are fished in the surface skim nothing like this happened, not until the fisher hooked a steelhead and then chances were the fish ran out of the hole and into the riffle, where there was no hazard.

Of course a few fish were lost on the wire, but there were so many fish around it was an easy matter to move down into another hole and find more. There wasn't enough barbed wire to line all the pools on the lower Ronde; besides, barbed wire was in scant supply, this being range land, with cows and horses roaming freely. Another kind of wire was in general use, and it didn't have barbs.

Jack Whitesel was one of the first to fly fish the Ronde, but Jack says Merlin Stidham may have fished it before him. And there was a barber from Spokane or Lewiston (it was never clear) and maybe a university professor from Pullman. And there was Thorson Bennett. Later, there was Ted Trueblood, Dub Price, Bill Nelson, Wes Drain, Ralph Wahl, Art Smith, Rick Miller, and that ace of aces, Lee Wulff. The stories that come back are remarkably similar.

They are about a river with many small fish that avidly take flies on the surface. It may have been the Ronde where Wulff applied the tactics he devised for dour Atlantic salmon to steelhead and proved that the tricks were just as effective, the fish similar. In fact, from those days

Wes Drain

of surface fishing on the Ronde may have derived most of the techniques for surface presentations that have become standard textbook fare in the West.

When I was "caught" fishing a sink tip the day I met Bill Nelson, he scoffed. It was inappropriate tackle, he told me. Worse, I would do much better with the floating line; a floating line on the Ronde was all I'd ever need.

I didn't believe him then, but I believe him now. I had to learn my lesson the hard way. It is my usual way.

Surface fishing the Ronde and other East Slope streams is easier than it sounds, but it may require an act of faith to the fisher who is used to taking his fish near the bottom and fishing for them with a sunk line, which is more difficult. If he has ever fished much for trout, he may have the wrong idea about what is involved. There is no hatch to be matched, no periodic feeding frenzy. Drag—long a problem for trouters—is not much of a consideration; sometimes it may be detrimental, but often it works to the fisher's advantage and is to be encouraged. Drag, encouraged? Well, if you can't beat it, join it.

Many good steelhead runs have a bubbly chop at the head and a strong rippling flow for most of their length. Hence it is nearly impossible for the fly to behave drag-free for more than a few feet of its journey. Anglers have found that a fish is just as likely to take a dragging fly as one that is behaving more conventionally. In fact, as the water slows, *only* a dragging fly is apt to induce a strike. So the amount of skill in presentation is minimized. This is good news.

It is good because the fly can simply be thrown to the current and left to work pretty much by itself. This must have been hard for early Westsiders to comprehend. There are reasons why Eastside steelhead are different from the fish found in Puget Sound rivers; they have been conditioned differently.

Fish in the Ronde have been in freshwater for months and for hundreds of miles of their journey. Their sea-feeding has long ago been shut off. Just as their bodies underwent the great biological transformation to smolts that prepared them for life in the salty sea, they have now reversed the chemical process and become acclimated to freshwater again. The change is tremendous. It is no wonder that they begin to key again to life in the river and regain their curiosity about what is being swept at them by the current.

Wulff has called this tendency to take food from the river a "conditioned reflex." It is probably as good a term as any, though not quite what psychologists mean when they discuss conditioning a person or an animal to respond to a stimulus through constant repetition. But it comes close. If the fish are as bored as Wulff says, and as restless in their lie holes, they will relieve the monotony from time to time by intercepting some bit of the dreck the river offers them. Sometimes the dreck includes insects—terrestials, too. It is as good an explanation as any for why steelhead react to surface flies, when they can gain no nourishment or sustenance from them.

To strike is natural for them. It is what they did as juveniles. Also, it is effortless, or near effortless, for a fish that has swam hundreds or perhaps thousands of miles in its lifetime. To move a few feet more to intercept a fly that looks like no special fly but like all flying creatures that find themselves impeded by being caught up in the surface tension of the river is no trouble. It might be considered "out of character" for a steelhead to pass up such a tidbit.

Wahl, Walt Johnson, Drain, Miller, and others from the west slopes of the Cascades had developed special skills in difficult wet-fly fishing in short-run streams that had relatively little insect life. A wet fly needed to sink and swim fetchingly; it had to break at a given point in the swing, while still sinking, so that it passed over the lie of an imaginary fish at just the right speed and depth. If the cast was handled correctly (and all the other conditions were right, too), a steelhead would take the fly and be hooked.

It was different here. To the East, all you had to do was throw your fly out in the current, keep it riding on the surface, and wait for the steelhead to supply the action. The particular behavior of the fly in the water didn't matter much. The more unnaturally it behaved the better. What you had to do was violate all the rules that made you successful as a wet-fly fisher to the West. Often this was hard to make yourself do.

A long cast, though, was helpful. Most of these men were excellent casters, having had to fling a wet-fly line consistent distances over fifty-five feet in order to reach the best holding water. To cast a full-floating line this far was a simple joy. It sailed out over the river, back and forth, and was a graceful thing to do or behold. At the end of a long tapered leader, the fly "turned over" and dropped to the surface. There it immediately began its long, enticing ride along the rip of the current. It was a beautiful thing to experience.

And it brought up fish from their depths. Oh, how it did. Often the catches were phenomenal. Rather than the West-side average of one true steelhead rise per day dry, a Ronde fisherman might have a dozen or more legitimate takes. He might have the hook catch enough to spin the reel handles in a high percentage of these rises. He might have on the reel seven or eight fish a day, and not have it considered unusual by men who had the same thing happen to them.

It was sport beyond comprehension, a week's normal fishing telescoped into a day's. And it might get even better. Reports of ten or a dozen fish to the beach were not uncommon. With fresh fish running up out of the Snake—to have several persons in a lineup have such excellent fishing and not detract much from the fishing of his neighbor was, well, extraordinary.

It still is. Each year there are days on the Ronde that duplicate those from the past, sensational days, days that men dream about but seldom realize elsewhere. Of course there are the ordinary days, too, the days with maybe one take, or less than one fish on the reel or brought to the beach. But you never know. One ordinary day may be followed by an exceptional one, or the exceptional day followed by the ordinary one, for no reason that anyone can discern. Both have happened to me, and I am still scratching my head in bewilderment.

It is exciting fishing. The fly rides merrily along its route, bouncing, bobbing, often twisting around in a half-circle on its leader. It whips, it pauses, it hurries along, it calms down. Somewhere in this great array of motion and behavior is a move that will trigger the steelhead's response. (Note, I do not say it is "conditioned," only that it is a response, a reaction. Let's stick with what we know for sure.) The fish comes arching up from its depths and snatches the fly.

We fumble a strike, amazed, and it turns out to be exactly the right thing to do, for the fish proves firmly hooked. We take full credit for our success, of course. (When you pay as much for your tackle as we do, we believe we have purchased our successes and own them. We believe this, even while we know better.)

The fish is a typical six-pound Ronde female and fights well if not excellently. It runs, it jumps, it takes out line, it gives back line to the spool. Soon it slides over on its side and proclaims it has had enough. A wild fish, it is ready for release. (If a hatchery fish, it is ready for release, too, for it doesn't recognize the difference in its origin, nor should we, most of the time.)

A surface fly on a floating line will draw a response from a high percentage of the fish running the river. I have no idea what this percentage is, or what "high" means, only that it is not unusual to hook fish after fish in such a situation. Of course it is possible that three or four hundred fish are passing through a run just upstream from the mouth, and if we hook three or four, that is not a high percentage; it is but one percent. It is possible that there are only thirty or forty fish in the run to result in the hooking of a similar number, which is ten percent, if my math holds, or there may be but ten or twelve fish holding briefly in the run, and if we hook the same number, it is indeed a very high percentage of the run. It is all.

Good fishing is not dependent upon catching a lot of steelhead out of a variable population in one or two pools fished on a given day's outing. Good fishing is exceeding the average, and that average for a good day's fishing is one fish to the beach; two fish to the beach is very good. Three fish hooked, if only two landed, is better yet. After this, the averages pale and words become superfluous.

Fishers, alas, are counters. We are numbers men. We do math in our heads while we fish. An example goes like this: we fish one long day and hook nothing. Forget it; it doesn't count. We fish another similar day; it is erased from our memory banks. We fish a morning and receive one strike, which we miss. We eat lunch. We set out again about one-thirty and fish until six-thirty. In that afternoon, we hook two fish and land them both.

What is our average? Why, it is a fish every two and one-half hours. If you don't believe me, just divide two into five. You see? How simple it is.

What is the ratio of fished hooked to fish landed? For the day it is two landed to three hooked. This is sixty-six percent. Those are good numbers, though unreal.

Good numbers are what we live for.

THIRTY-TWO

There is a familiar story fishers tell about a man who hooked a fish and lost it. He saw it jump before it came off the hook. How big was the fish? "Twelve and a half pounds." We all nod thoughtfully. Nobody challenges him.

To see a fish in the air and judge its weight to within half a pound is ordinary fare for steelhead fishers. We have taken a vow never to shout, "Liar, liar, pants on fire," to each other. We nod, stroke our chins, avert our eyes, and wait for the opportunity to tell one ourselves.

I have never questioned Jerry Wintle about the following; I wouldn't dare. If I did, he'd never listen to me again. He'd never play the game of "You listen. Now it's my turn."

The last day of the season three or four years ago, Jerry hopped in his boat and powered off to a nameless hole we'll call Larson's on the middle Skagit. Somebody went with him, not his wife Jean but probably Dave Winters, an old friend. They had had a few drinks. Just before dark, Jerry hooked a huge steelhead. We all know the Skagit has monster steelhead because we've all hooked some and landed a few. Jerry played and beached his; they measured it along the impregnated nine-foot bamboo fly rod he invariably uses. They agreed on where the fish came in relation to the guides on the rod.

They motored back to the camp at Rockport. They brought out a tape and measured from the butt to the agreed-on mark.

It was forty-eight inches. (Actually, it was an inch or so more, but they subtracted that bit, believing nobody would believe a fish forty-nine and two-thirds inches long. Ah, but would they believe one an inch or two shorter? Not likely, either.) Nobody doubted it, publicly or privately. Nor did I.

I was putting together an issue of *The Osprey* (a newsletter for steelheaders interested in the preservation of wild steelhead, which I edited) and decided to verify with a reporter's thoroughness the fish's length. I called the apartment in Vancouver, B.C., where Jerry and Jean live when they aren't camped by some river renowned for its wild steelhead. Jerry was out (fishing), but Jean was at home.

"Forty-eight inches and some," she said, not blinking. I know: It's hard to see somebody not blink over the telephone.

Now Jerry has a reputation for honesty, along with catching fish. Dutifully I reported it in the newsletter. They took no girth measure; seldom do we ever, we are so anxious not to man-handle our fish further and get it back into the water after the longitudinal survey. But even giving the fish an average latitudinal reading, the steelhead would have weighed fifty pounds. That is a world's record by many pounds, including fish taken by gillnets.

Do I doubt Jerry's veracity? Of course not. Do I want him to doubt mine, when I catch one a full inch longer?

THIRTY-THREE

One person I enjoy running into on the Wenatchee each fall is Dick Sylbert. Once he took a thirteen-pound fish on a dry fly; so have I. We have this and other things in common.

Dick makes movies. He has been production designer for many of Warren Beatty's fine movies, including "Reds," when he lived in Europe (Paris and Spain, mostly) and got to meet a number of writers whom I admire. I love to get Dick talking about writers and their idiosyncracies. I also enjoy talking about the movies themselves, which I remember vividly. I have a vast collection of videotapes of movies, many whose production was designed by Dick. In fact, I accumulate them.

Dick Sylbert

I do not know anything about production design, except that he has a twin brother, Paul, who does the same thing. Dick has his own company. I gather that they are responsible for the sets, the location, the order in which the scenes are shot (for maximum efficiency and economy), and the general ambience of the movie. Dick did *Chinatown*, with Roman Polanski, in which the golden-brown atmosphere of rural, long-ago Los Angeles was carried to artform status. Dick would have made *The Two Jakes,* which was its sequel, except something more critical called him away. No, it wasn't fly fishing.

When I run into Dick, I always want to talk movies. I want to ask him questions and get answers from the inside, from the horse's mouth. He wants to talk about fly fishing for steelhead. I can always do that. Well, nearly. It's not often I can talk to Warren Beatty's cohort and learn the vital facts of life, such as what is the key to Beatty's fantastic success with women? I mean, what does he *do*? Instead, Dick wants to know what fly I'm getting them on.

After one fine week the Wenatchee was hit by a deluge and he and I and guide Joe Butorac sat in a motel in Cashmere, drinking Bud and watching old movies on the American Movie Channel, which came free with the lodging, waiting for the river to clear. Dick, who is a little older than I, has a long and illustrious career. He began in New York City, and you can make out the sound of the Bronx in his voice without listening too hard. He made movies there before he went out to L.A.

One of his came on the air. (I'm sorry, Dick, but I've forgotten its name.) It was done in black and white and was of the *genre* (see how easily I'm able to bandy the words around?) keyed to the use of those colors or non-colors. He pointed out some of his special effects, and Joe and I whistled appreciatively. The movie was one of the *noire*. Men were tough whiskey-drinkers, and the women had no androgenous qualities. There were guns and kissing and beating people up. It was great fun. The river remained out.

Then the World Series of baseball began. Since Dick was from NYC, he had all the batting averages implanted in his skull at birth. Me, I could hardly fake it. Questions about movies now seemed about as relevant as questions about childbirth. I sat with my questions in my mouth, unspoken. Meanwhile, bats were being swung, hits beaten out, Texas leaguers missed, and bases stolen. I don't remember the teams, either, but they were the best of 1991.

On the twin double beds with which all motels come today was spread an array of fishing tackle whose value was about three thousand dollars. There was Dick's 3-3/4 St. George, the kind no longer made, and bought while there were a few languishing in stores to replace the cherished one stolen from his home on the North Fork. The rods were Sages, and there were fine Orvis bags and Dick's terribly soiled khaki cap, with the FFF silver pin twinkling on its front.

Flies—so many of them. Joe Butorac is a professional tier, and if you go into a store and buy a handful of superb steelhead flies, chances are they will be his. And Wheatley fly boxes, jammed to the gunnels. Neoprene waders, gruff wading shoes, cleated overshoes, slick rain jackets. Reel spools with new, bright floating fly lines on them in rainbow colors. In short, all the accoutrements of our odd sport and obsession.

One of Dick's favorite flies is the Black Squirrel. (See Fly Plate Number 7.) The one he sent me is housed in my private collection. Its tail is fox squirrel, the body silver-tinsel-core-ribbed black chenille, the body hackle black saddle, the front hackle missing, the wing fox squirrel again, tied body length and short of the tail. Later, he sent me a black version. It reminds me of Tom Crawford's fly, Bush Baby, and the two of them form a pair to draw to.

Dick and Joe had been eating at two restaurants, alternating them, the one offering only pizza and the other ordinary country food served in volume. I told them about Barney's and took them there. It was taco night. Now, tacos are not too sustaining to men who fish hard, or who have drunk a lot of beer while watching old movies or baseball games, but it was all the tavern offered, that night. It could have been worse, for the following day they had their full menu back, but the evening was dedicated to a sing-a-long. We might have had to warble for our supper.

We drank more beer, slower, and gorged on tacos. They were cheap, we called it dinner. We talked fishing and baseball. It was Dick's vacation, so we still didn't talk movies. (They weren't on the menu, either, you might say.) It was a wonderful evening. We parted about midnight and I was half looped.

They spent the night in a warm motel, I in my tent trailer. It was October, the rains had stopped, the temperature got down to about sixteen degrees. I had trouble in the morning getting myself out of my warm sleeping bag and into the air, where everything remained frozen. There was no special reason to rise, anyway, since the river ran bank-high and carried a brown cast.

Dick has this particular habit of arriving by air on the same night as the river goes out. I don't know how he does it. He and Joe once rented a house in Wenatchee for the season; another time they did the same thing in Rockport, on the Skagit. These were clever moves. I think they were carry-overs from Dick's work and something he was used to doing, as they say, on location. Both times the river immediately went out.

One season the river ran bone dry for weeks and only rose a couple of inches when the ag diversion ended. Fishing wasn't bad. Then a storm moved in from Seattle. (In Cashmere, all storms have their roots in Seattle, you see. We are called "206ers," after our area-code.) It rained in the night and all the next day. Dick was flying in from some sound-alike place like Belgrade or Bangkok or Brussels. Late in the afternoon, the river began to rise, though the color held good. At full dark it was lapping at the brush and still lifting an inch an hour. I drove to the motel in town a block from Barney's. Dick was arriving near midnight, Joe told me.

In the morning I checked the river and was astonished at its full force. As it was too high to fish even at my Camp Pool, I ate breakfast and drove into town to their motel. Dick and Joe were gearing up to go out on the water. I think Joe knew what shape the river was in. Dick's enthusiasm, however, could not be contained. I was not about to utter a discouraging word and Joe was too depressed to. I moved aside as they hurried through the doorway to the car that would carry them to the first pool, one brimming over. My car was packed with my portable gear and I was ready to head for home. The river would not clear for four or five days, I knew.

Dick had three days away from location. My heart went out to him. His cardinal joy was the floating line and surface fly. Like Bill Nelson, he didn't like to fish any other way. I know how he felt. If fish will take on top, why go after them near the bottom? What would you rather have, one fish on top or three down deep?

Don't be too quick to answer.

THIRTY-FOUR

Which brings me back to the Ronde. Though I have repeatedly written about it, and tried to express my great affection, I have not done it justice, and I know this. It may be the most beloved river this side of the Madison. It is not hard to understand why. It is so beautiful, with its rocky desert canyons and sparkling riffles. It is just big enough to require respect, while being small enough to wade in not all, but enough, places.

Don't misunderstand. I am married to the North Fork and the Wenatchee (if you will indulge me one more fatuous analogy) is my long-time mistress. Then the Grande Ronde is who I keep returning to for a one-night stand or possibly a weekend tryst. When the name of the Ronde is spoken, my eyes shine and my mind goes wandering off to remembered good times. It does for many.

I've written of how Bill Nelson scoffed at my sinking line and told me all that was necessary was one that floated and how I ignored him and had to have that lesson driven home to me by experience. Well, Nelson learned the lesson from Dub Price.

The rule of life (and fly fishing) is "Pass it on." You must do so, however unwillingly, for it is part of the code. You accept the code the first time you step into a river.

Walt "Dub" Price is an Everett angler. He is a commercial artist and the first time I met him I was working for Safeco, buying art for stuff I was writing that had to do with selling insurance and mutual funds. We had no designers or artists of our own and had to go out into the community to find them. This was fun. I had heard of Dub as a fisherman and, naturally, sought him out. He immediately turned the job over to a colleague. He preferred to draw and paint.

In my home on the North Fork I had a "reject" painting done by Dub. It resided in one bedroom, across from the foot of the bed. He gave it to me, but refused to sign it. (Over the years I've asked him to put his name on it, but he refuses, always with a steely look. I think I understand. It is not his best work. What he should have done is destroyed the painting, not given it to me, but it had enough merit for him not to want to burn it. It is now the property of my neighbor Joe Bly, who is a fellow club member of his.)

I like the painting. It is of an intrepid fly fisher standing by a shrunken river whose banks are thick with snow. On a hot day I can cool off just by looking at it. Dub has fished the North Fork, but is not known as one of its premier steelhead anglers. He's done much better on its sea-run cutthroat.

On the Grande Ronde he was king for a while. Maybe it was his cut-throat-trout tactics that did it for him, I don't know. Anyway, he and Bill Nelson were camped on the Ronde and Nelson (like I, that day) was fishing a full sinking line, one of those new ones called Hi-Density. This places the scene in the mid-Sixties, the Ronde just entering its long decline, but fish still ran up from the Snake when the fall weather turned cool and there was rain to raise the river. Dub told Nelson to put away his heavy fiberglass rod and try Dub's light-weight one, which was equipped with a floating double-taper and a slender fly tied the "grease [*sic*] line" style. Nelson, a good fisher (as are all anglers who took their basic training on the North Fork) hooked fish after fish in a pool which had given him no action earlier, fished wet. He enthusiastically cried out, "This is glorified trout fishing."

Exactly.

Dub has written about those days in *The Creel, The Bulletin of The Fly fisher's Club of Oregon.* The word "bulletin" is a coy understatement. *The Creel* is a handsome journal that came out once or twice a year during its heyday. Lately it has sunk into obscurity, what with the great increase in publishing costs and the long production time a quality publication requires. One special issue was published in the early 1990s; that may be it, for its originators have aged and do not have the energy and dedication they once had. And some have died. This includes Thorson Bennett, the Grand Master of the Ronde. [I am grateful to *The Creel* for much of the material that follows and have quoted and abstracted from it shamelessly.]

In fact, Bennett was still gathering materials for his contribution to *The Creel* when he died in 1974. The journal published a memorial issue, and in it Bob Wethern wrote, with his usual precision and flair: "The joy of knowing Thorson H. Bennett when he still was the leonine-appearing master steelheader of his Grande Ronde River birthplace makes comment now on his passing, at a time when his home river also seems to face extinction, painfully difficult."

Bennett also had a difficulty—it was completing his writing assignments. *The Creel* had the distinction of bringing out the best in fishers who were not known to be writers and inspiring them to produce good prose. His delay was compounded by his interpreting his mission as being to trace out the history of the early days of La Grande, Oregon. This consumed much of his time. Of this search, he wrote, in the year before his death: "I have traveled many miles and written as many letters in my search for very pertinent data and factual information regarding both my father's and my mother's families, early pioneers to the Oregon Country which would be relevant to my proposed story for *The Creel*, and have collected a few prizes for my efforts.

" . . . I have been promised a picture of the river ferry that my Great Grandfather Jake P. Sturgill operated across the Grande Ronde, in the early days of Troy. My mother's first cousin, Marjorie Weaver, 86, whose mother was one of J. P.'s daughters, awarded my trip to Spokane with a picture of him!

". . . I greatly fear the halcyon days of the Grande Ronde are over, when that marvelous river yielded up its fish so generously. The 1972 season was a warning; this fall it became a reality." Bennett lived only ten more months into that "reality" and missed the resurgence of the Ronde which, however, was the result of hatchery plants and the surviving spawn of hatchery fish. It would not have pleased him.

He was very much tied to the country. In 1965, he wrote: "My grandfather settled Enterprise, Oregon, and my dad was born there in 1874. I was delivered to him at Elgin in 1903, not far from the banks of my favorite river, which I've fished most of a lifetime."

He makes it sound like the Ronde was his favorite river even before he was born, which is just barely possible, I suppose, for a "born" steelheader. It sounds a little like—in those days of raging patriarchy—his father produced him by a supreme act of will, with his mother making little contribution to his deliverance. But there is little doubt she exists, and he is fond of her, for when Bennett is tracing out his family tree, her side of the family is important, too. He speaks of collecting important materials from his mother's sister while on a trip to Los Angeles: ". . . her dad was Captain William Booth, U.S. Calvary, who was stationed in Chief Joseph's territory. Many of my Grandfather Bennett's descendants, first white settlers in the Wallowas, are still living in Eastern Oregon and Washington."

Like many fabled steelheaders, Bennett was tall, august, austere. Unless he knew you, he was not glad to run into you on "his" river, and there was no mistaking his attitude from his demeanor. As with other legends, it is hard to sort out the truth from fable. Dub Price has it that Bennett usually fished with full sinkers or sink tips and used those early fiberglass rods that were yellow and had thick butts. (If you want one, I'll give one to each of the first three people who form a line.) He didn't cast far; he had no need to, for the fish were right at his feet.

Others have Bennett fishing a floating line. Frank Cammack, who ran into him at the mouth of the Wind in 1960, says he was fishing huge white bucktails, which he greased with mucilin so they would float. (Bucktail invariably floats with a little grease; it is the old floating lines that began to sink quickly and needed flies that would resist the tendency of the line to drag them under.) Giving Cammack "a little lesson in fishing" is a standard steelheader's put-down and Bennett was no more tactful than any other accomplished angler who sends a neophyte scurrying back to the trout stream.

It is interesting to study Bennett for style in how he almost did this to Cammack. It combines extreme politeness with extreme arrogance: "My name is Thorson Bennett. Would you be offended if I stepped in the river just above you and fished the water directly in front of you?" The usual answer to this (at least from me, if you want to try me on it) is, "Yes, I would be offended. Please go somewhere else until I am gone."

Instead, Cammack told him he was welcome to try, "but indicated I doubted there were any steelhead in the shallow riffle." This man keeps compounding his mistakes. To put it another way, he keeps asking for comeuppance. Bennett is the one to deliver it.

It took but three dry-fly floats of the big, white bucktail over the gut before "a bright steelhead appeared in an aerial exit to the Columbia River." Nice phrasing. "Excuse me," the preoccupied Thorson said, "I have a steelhead on and would like to slip by you."

(Once Jerry Wintle said something much like this to Rick Miller on the North Fork's Elbow Hole and Miller stepped deeper into the hole. This necessitated an interesting series of hip checks, while Jerry followed his fish downstream and, eventually, to the beach. The two men have not spoken since and thirty years have passed.)

Cammack stepped aside and, "properly humbled," watched Bennett land the six pounder, club it on the head, and carry it daintily up the beach on his fingertips.

Cammack invited Bennett to step back in the hole and repeat the act. This is tantamount to trying to choke your enemy to death by serving him prime ribs. Instead—and here Bennett evidences the style that others keep alluding to—he showed Cammack the "puffball" fly and asked him if he had one. Cammack said no. Bennett offered his and coached Cammack from the beach into the darkness, but no further steelhead rose. They talked till midnight. Bennett asked him if he could be back at sunrise. He was pretty sure he could get him into a fish then.

Cammack writes, "Rushing back to Portland I tied three 'puffballs,' slept two hours, then rushed back to Thorson's camp for a quick breakfast before daylight."

Bennett inspected Cammack's flies. He said they would have to be greased a lot to float. It was not the highest compliment.

Shortly after daylight Cammack hooked a fish, but lost it on its third jump. Bennett slipped into the water and clobbered a five pounder. Then the morning fishing was over. Bennett, Cammack, and Bennett's wife, Beth, picked blackberries and chatted about steelheading. Bennett invited him to fish on *his* Grande Ronde with him. Cammack says he regrets he never took him up on the offer and then it was too late. Bennett was dead.

One year Dub Price and Bennett fished together and Bennett briefly forsook his huge bucktails for a tiny greased-line fly that Price had given him years ago. He caught a nice steelhead on it and Price took it as the finest compliment. He regrets not having "thanked" Bennett aloud. This is the kind of reverence the man inspired. It is hard to find another like him.

Price describes him thus: "In a first impression—and forever—Thorson was a striking man. He was tall and lean. His bony frame was topped with a long angular face and a full head of wild hair. I thought to myself, here is a softly quiet and gray John Carradine (the stage and movie actor).

"Thorson's hat brim was stuck full of large flies, hackles of gray and brown and wings of squirrel, fox, deer and bear hair. They were enormous, especially compared to the spare greased line flies I gave him. Oh, I told him where the fish lay and where to wade. . ." It wasn't till later that Price learned that Bennett had fished the river for decades and knew its every nook.

In years to come, Thorson, Price, Nelson and many others came to look forward to the communal camp annually set up on the lower reaches of the Ronde. Bennett began to slow; often he stayed in camp and waited to hear about the luck of his friends when they returned from a morning's fishing. He might suit up, late in the day, and wade gingerly out into a favorite riffle, where he would not move his feet and repeat the same cast, over and over. His friends greeted each other with concerned frowns.

In 1973, he did not make roll call. Fishing was poor, the trip hardly worth it. The next year the river closed as a conservation measure to protect its dwindling wild-fish run, Bennett died the same year. The river went unfished. As a result of hatchery bolstering with big money set aside for this purpose as part of the Upper Columbia and Snake river restoration projects for dam mitigation, the runs began to build again and the numbers of returning fish to be large enough to allow limited fishing for them, at first on a catch-and-release basis and later as hatchery-keep only.

Some of the original anglers return annually. The numbers of these veterans grows smaller, year by year. They are being replaced by a new breed—men and women who "can't remember when." As a whole the younger ones are better fishers. They have a more holistic understanding of how a riverine ecosystem works and its needs for constant vigilance.

Releasing all or most of their catch of steelhead is a reflex action with them. (Wulff might say it was a "conditioned" reflex, and he would not be far off the mark.) The politeness of the "new" angler probably exceeds that of Thorson Bennett's generation. The number of meaningful lessons bestowed on a neophyte is less today. A genuine politeness and consideration abounds. Some of it is remembered politeness, to be sure, for crowded water still shortens tempers and leads to angry thoughts, sometimes words, rarely actions, but the friendliness of anglers and their willingness to share information with well-meaning strangers is greater than in the memorable past. And that is good. It is all for the betterment of our sport.

THIRTY-FIVE

Fishing with a floating line is also an effective way of catching sea-run cutthroat, a trout that goes to sea and returns to feed and spawn. These fish—and the ways of fishing for them—are similar to "seatrout" fishing for browns that visit the sea to put on growth in the rivers of Great Britain, Argentina, Norway, and elsewhere, though ours grow nowhere near so big. Most of ours run between nine and 18 inches, with a fairly large number in the two- and three-pound class.

My friend Walt Johnson holds the state record for a sea-run cutthroat that weighed nearly six pounds. It was a huge fish and was caught in saltwater; though Walt is mum about where he catches his fish (and expects me to be, too), chances are it was off the beach in Hood Canal, at the bottom of Puget Sound and on the Olympic Peninsula side. Walt seriously fishes the North Fork for cutts in the fall and when their season overlaps with the steelhead gives them priority. A fisher can learn a lot by watching Walt fish with his small rods and flies that often go down to midge size.

Not so serious, I usually pass cutts by in favor of pursuing dour steelhead. Often this proves a mistake from the standpoint of catching fish. Meanwhile, friends are scoring—and scoring big—on cutts fresh in from the sea.

Thanks to protective measures regulated by the Department of Wildlife and advanced by Curt Kraemer and the late Dave Round of the Federation of Fly Fishers, the numbers of sea-run cutthroat in Puget Sound streams have increased remarkably in the past decade. Fishing for them provides a pleasant diversion from the year-round pursuit of steelhead and is a refreshing change. It takes me back to first principles. Practically all of us began on trout, and it is trout fishing we ought to keep in mind when fishing with the floating line under low-water conditions for both steelhead and cutts.

This year we had a good spring flow that persisted into mid-summer. Rivers throughout the West stayed high into July and began their annual drop late, providing good escapement of wild steelhead into their headwater sanctuaries. Then, in August, the rivers dropped steadily, reaching a low at the end of the month below their record drought-levels of recent years. Just when we thought the North Fork could go no lower it did, and the Wenatchee remained so low through September that my favorite pools were no fun to fish—with incredible slack and vast backwaters. What was worse, few steelhead ascended.

For the first time I turned my attention to sea-run cutts, and in the process I learned a thing or two. What's more, I had fun.

The cutts this year were running smaller than usual, but there were many more than in past years. Good, at least for me, for I am inexpert when it comes to catching trout. If I once knew anything, I've forgotten it all. What I had to do was offer myself up to the trout and see what they would teach me.

With sea-run cutthroat fishing, first you have to find them, as is the case with all anadromous fish. They may be anywhere and nowhere. The river may be scarce, one day, and contain fairly large concentrations the next. To learn which is the case, you must venture out and try to establish contact.

Often (but not always) cutts give themselves away by actively feeding. Steelhead do not do this. To find cutts, you must learn to tell their feeding splashes from those of salmon sporting around a pool, for in odd-numbered years humpies have a misleading soft splash that looks very much like a feeding trout. Fry and fingerlings are always ringing the pools in the evening and splashing noisily about while feeding. Cutthroats feed similarly, taking food softly, daintily, on or near the surface, and other times splashing in a manner that startles and stirs the imagination of any fisher who hears or sees it. Often they will chase a fly and hit it hard.

Cutts tend to live long and grow slowly. They remain in their headwater nurseries for the first year of life and move downstream only after it is past.

Thus, a one-year fish may be only a couple of inches long; a two-year-old a little over four inches; a three-year-old maybe six or seven inches; a four-year-old just over eight, which used to be the legal keep size in many enclosed waters, but no longer is. (It has wisely been raised.) By age five they are about ten inches in length. Often they do not go to sea until they are three or four years old and even then do not increase their growth rate much.

Though nobody knows exactly where they go at sea, evidence is overwhelming (low growth rate alone would indicate this) that they do not migrate far to areas of food abundance but instead remain near their estuaries and range only a short distance. Many are caught in saltwater and this has become a popular sport fishery necessary to regulate with size and number limits. Fish biologists operate under the sound principle that it is vital for the continuation of the race of a species that an individual be protected until it has spawned once. A minimum size for cutts has been established at 14 inches, with a limit of two, but fish can be caught and released up until the angler has had his fill, or has found two cutts large enough to grease up the pan.

I think a sea-run cutt of, say, sixteen or eighteen inches is a wonderful fish and am always divided between wanting to bring home a pair or releasing them, a quandary which pursues me up into the restricting darkness. I grew up in that generation of men who believed they should be able to bring home sufficient fish and game to provide for their families. I took pride in the fact that my small family—if I extended it only slightly—numbered seven and I could "provide" fish for them all. With steelhead in the early days of hatchery abundance, this was easily accomplished. My family shrunk in size, just as the Indian nets began taking the bulk of hatchery fish and anglers were left with only the wild fish that had to be set free. This was fine with me.

When my mother was in a retirement home, I once was so confident of my prowess that I offered to supply the residence with enough winter hatchery steelhead for their dining room, only to be told that all meat and fish had to be federally inspected before they could accept it; this nicely helped end my days of unconscionable slaughter.

A big cutt is an old fish by most trout and all steelhead standards. Accordingly, it is to be respected, venerated. I find this easy to do. A big, feeding cutt is a marvelous fish, an efficient engine; it feeds nearly all the time, for our rivers and nearby saltchuck are not rich with food. It hits hard and fights strongly. If you find sea-runs, chances are they will be feeding and in a hitting mood, sometimes they get choosy, though. While they are not so easily frightened or put down as steelhead are, they can be disturbed and their feeding routines interrupted.

We almost always fish for cutts with a floating line. People call this dry fly, even if it isn't. Usually it involves the use of small attractor flies that swim just under the surface with a variety of actions induced by the angler's retrieve. Not surprisingly, the same kinds of flies that catch big sea-going browns in Europe will catch our cutts. One big difference is that we do not fish for cutts at night. (But probably somebody will try this and learn that it is effective, and then everybody will start doing it, to the exclusion of day-light fishing.) Fishing for cutts is best on a cloudy day, or when the sun is off the water, but fishing is often pretty good under a bright sun.

The fish love slack water (of which, in fall, there is plenty) and bank pockets where there are natural obstructions, such as logs and drooping branches. These make casting difficult, and often a risked throw to a tight spot along the bank results in hanging up the fly and leader in some branch-es, where they are lost.

It seems to me that small flies tend to remain on the surface and not fish right unless they are weighted. I used to have disdain for weighted nymphs and wets but no longer do, for anglers too pure to do this usually resort to heavy hooks instead, which produce similar results: they get the fly beneath the surface film where it will swim, rather than hop in and out of the top layer. Besides, on a long, light leader and floating line, a small hook—say, an ordinary eight or a 10-16 Wilson—is not going to sink very deep, even if it is weighted.

Also not surprisingly, steelhead flies will catch sea-run browns. James Waltham, in his book *Sea Trout Flies* (Black, London, 1988), visited the Deschutes River in Oregon and fished for steelhead, which he likened to "seatrout," not Atlantic salmon. He brought back dressings of our stan-dards and fished them successfully for anadromous browns. I and others dress many of our cutthroat flies from patterns long effective for British seatrout, so it is indeed a small world, and in more ways than I had thought.

Partridge and Orange, Teal and Silver (and Blue), March Brown, Teal and Red, etc., are all good cutthroat flies. My favorite, however, is Al Knudsen's Mallard Spider, which could as easily be called Mallard and Yellow, for that is what it is. Tying such flies requires the ability to "work small," which is not one of my traits; also, breast feathers from ducks have curved quills that are difficult to wind on. The fibers of the feathers them-selves have a decided twist that is both their advantage and their drawback. To get the curl to turn in the right direction requires experimentation and determination in doubling a hackle, but the effort is worth it.

The procedure of doubling a feather so that both sides of the fibers slant in the same direction and when tied in are sloped backwards at a decided angle is important. There seems to be three main ways of accomplishing this: (1) reversing the quill and rubbing it hard against an object with a sharp edge, such as a fingernail, etc., (2) dry stroking, with the fibers first turned at right angles to the quill, (3) wet stroking, using water, spit, martini (Poul Jorgensen's method), etc., to thoroughly wet down the fibers so they can be turned and matted back on the same side. The purpose in all instances is the same; it is to get all the hackle fibers turned to the same side, slanted prettily, and not wrapped under each other or facing forward. With the pronounced curl in duck feathers this is more difficult than, say, with saddle hackles, but it can be done. Firmness and persistence is the order of the day. Tying the feather in tip first helps a lot, too.

Usually two turns of the hackle will do for a sparsely dressed fly. Having said this, I am sure I give more than half my cutthroat flies three or four turns, if the feather is long enough. And I have been know to cut off unruly fibers, bunch them, and tie them in either winged or beard style. This makes for a neater fly, though it docs not swim so fetchingly.

On the North Fork, anglers have a tradition of saying that they are going out for cutthroat, then returning with a big grin and a summer steelhead. The question is, were they really after cutthroat or steelhead? The answer may be ambiguous, the attitude truly ambivalent. I fish the swift part of a pool for steelhead, and the slow part with a small fly and slow retrieve for cutts, which should attract no normal steelhead, but I am often surprised by a cutthroat take in swift, steelheady water. Not so often I get a steelhead take in slack water, or while retrieving my fly at a slow pace—tediously slow, both for me and the steelhead.

The other day while fishing a riffling dry fly for steelhead, a cutt took hard in the fast water along the far bank. This was unusual in itself, but what followed was special. The fish fought a dogged fight, much like an old brown, and bulldogged deep, never jumping or splashing on the surface until I brought him near. Then I saw a brilliant wine-colored stripe running well below his median line. This was no rainbow, though, nor did the fish perform the usual cutthroat acrobatics and make jagged, slashing runs that never seem to cease. Instead, he slogged it out.

The fish was about a foot long and olive brown in color. (Most sea-run cutts are silvery green.) I took it in hand and studied it, a probable male, prior to releasing it. He looked unlike any sea-run I had ever caught; what he *did* look like was a Montana blackspotted cutthroat. Towards the tail he had numerous dark speckled spots, but these disappeared at the shoulder and were replaced by solid pigmentation. I turned the fish over and saw his bright cutthroat slashes; then I unpinned him and hurried him back into the water. I did not think to look to see if he had a clipped adipose fin, denoting a hatchery fish. (I think not.) I call the fish a "he" simply because of its dark coloration and bright belly slash. This seemed to me unmistakably male and often the sign of a spawning fish, but the soonest my fish could have spawned was three months off.

Most cutts look and behave consistently. A slow retrieve is often best, with the line being drawn in about as gently as it will come and still be moving. I think that what happens is the trout follows and over-runs the fly, then is faced with a dilemma: does it turn away, or does it simply continue and sup what it was chasing? In the latter case, the take is soft, but the good fisher will sense it and strike accordingly. Many times the fish simply hooks itself on the turn. This is similar to nymph fishing and I suppose a strike indicator would be useful.

On other days, and in order to cover a lot of water fast, a quick, jerking retrieve may be best, the fly literally popping along in the water. Mike Kinney likes this type of retrieve and a fly with a lot of action or motion; to achieve it, he often ties the hackle slanting *forward*, not backwards. I've fished this way often enough to know the strike is commonly a violent one. The careless fisher will pop off three-pound test tippet. The trick is to strike quickly but not hard. It is a kind of pull-push action, and is not unlike how I react to the strike of a dragging steelhead fly.

When you've found some cutthroats, the fishing is often fast and exciting. Once this year I walked into a slack-water stretch I've seen Walt fishing in years past. There was no sign of fish feeding. I hooked and landed two nice cutthroats of about 13 and 15 inches on four casts. (I then cast repeatedly to adjacent water for half an hour, without another take.)

I'm not good at sea-run cutthroat fishing, I know, and have friends who are skilled. Russ Miller is one. To become similarly talented will take years of dedication and I'm not sure I have the patience, not when there may be steelhead around, but more and more each year I go after them. I don't catch a lot of them, according to popular scores I hear about, but my few thrill me. To fish and fish carefully, and have no takers, but then to find a new piece of water that has numerous cutts feeding and striking, is a great experience. The action exceeds what a steelheader is used to.

And the trouting problems to be overcome are endlessly fascinating. The other night I found my usual cutthroat water empty—if it was not, I could not get them to take after having run through my whole bag of tricks, including some tiny nymphs. Then I caught a cutt that went all of nine inches. *Nine inches?*

That's right, and I knew at once what it was and put the fish on the reel. I played a nine-inch fish off the spool like a beginner might. (Or an old steelheader.) The fish fought about as well as a nine-inch trout can fight and leapt high in the air three times and came close to taking line off the spool, but only tightened it to the drag point.

Farther down in the pool, under a spreading bigleaf maple, where there was a stump on the bank and some bone-dry limbs jutting out from the stump, a big cutt was rising noticeably. He made a loud, slurping sound each time he took food from the surface. I don't know what he was eating. There were some small butterflies around that looked like moths, but I don't think they were what he was after. I saw no caddis, nor nymphing activity or cast-off larval shucks. O how I wanted that big cutt.

On my way downriver I cast my big Knudsen Spider into the snaggy hole in which he lay, risking a hang-up on the limb hanging in front of it. I cast and cast again, each time risking the fly and tippet, knowing that it was getting dark fast and I had only enough light and time left in the day to tie on one more fly and leader if I lost these. I moved on and took another small cutt, which I played on the strip, forcing myself to do so—a real trouter for the moment. Finally at dusk I walked up past the snag, eyeing it craftily and not looking at it directly because it continued to frustrate and challenge me. Slurp, said the big, hungry cutt. It was not for the first time.

I reentered the water as quietly as I could, considering that I was in a hurry and it was late-late, and began casting hard to the same location. My casts came far short of the target. Angrily I whipped out more line and threw it farther. I lashed the water, I knew, but it couldn't be helped. The fly was the same yellow spider: it was too dark to change and, besides, I was determined to make that cutt take this pattern.

I risked all and forced my cast under the spreading bigleaf—and did not hook the limb. I slammed my cast right up against the stump; I did this three times straight without losing my fly, giving it three different retrieves, each as seductive as I could make it. I had put that fish down and knew it. He would not honor my presence with another rise, not even a meager one.

He may be there still. I left the pool and the river. I continue to remember him and his cutthroat mockery of me and my inadequate skills. Each time I pass the stump in the future I will think of him. Evermore.

Thirty-six

When Moe shows up, the season for autumn steelhead has begun. The river may be the Grande Ronde, the Methow, the Clearwater, the Snake, or the Wenatchee. Chances are, it will be the Wenatchee. We both love this river, and I annually greet him with mixed feelings, for he has a way of filling up my favorite pools when I want them most to myself, though he is a pleasant fellow, very dedicated to our sport, and a pleasure to talk to.

He is Maurice E. McGuckin. I met him years ago, coming out of the public showers at the county park at Monitor. There for a succession of quarters you can take a shower for as long as you can afford one. It is good for washing away the accumulated grit and sweat and stink of a week's fishing, when the temperature rarely dips below eighty.

Moe has short white hair (a crewcut?) and full white beard. He's hard to miss. He is a professional steelhead fly fisher. For a living he does drywall; to do it he must travel around the state.

Moe lives in a van, which he has equipped for barebones living. There he cooks, eats, ties flies, sleeps. There is just enough room inside for one. Often his wife, Tina, is with him. Like many of us today, we marrieds have our own cars, so that we can come and go with separate abandon. But sleep and live they do in the van. I, in my tent trailer, do much the same thing, but mine is semi-permanently installed in its riverside niche accorded me by Lawrence Peterson's generosity, and I am not inclined to move it. Moe moves his rig at will, which makes him more mobile than me. He can go any place steelhead might be. And he does.

Moe is such a determined steelheader that he makes me appear half-hearted in comparison; and lazy. He is usually in his bunk by nine, up at four, even if it doesn't get light enough to fish until six. He is the type to rise singing, eager to begin the new day. Meanwhile I go to bed late, with a few beers and maybe a movie under my belt, and get up at a gentlemanly eight or nine.

My orchardist and fishing friends laugh at me; they are all early risers, too. They are like Moe, in this regard. I try to be on the river by ten. Okay, by ten-thirty. By then Moe is taking his first break.

If nobody is around and challenging him for the pool he has decided to fish, he may take a mid-morning rest. He may even nap, but he keeps half an eye cocked for an invader. Sleeping so slightly, his waders on, his rod by his side, his fly carefully tied to his tippet with its invariable Duncan knot, Moe is as able to spring into action as a young Doberman Pincer. And with about as much charm and grace.

I don't want to make it sound like Moe is my Nemesis, even if he is. Moe reduces my effectiveness on a given pool, on a certain day, by at least fifty percent. Yet if Moe does not show up, and I know he is in the neighborhood, I begin to wonder if I am missing out on something vital. Is he catching fish by the numbers down at Horse Lake or up behind the fruit packers at Dryden? Shouldn't I be there, too—especially since I've twice gone through our favorite pools and touched not a thing? Or did he prick them all earlier, while I slept?

Moe says his wife fishes, but I've never seen her cast a line. He tells me about all the big trout they catch in some secret lake near Spokane. Tina is a dark, attractive, slender woman; she has fine features and a quiet, friendly, intelligent manner. I once thought she was East Indian; then I thought she was Colville Indian, Moe tells me she is Hawaiian. She keeps to herself but is approachable. She is always reading a book, which is a more useful thing to do than casting for steelhead by the hour—especially when you don't keep them to eat. The first time I met her, she was reading David James Duncan's, *The River Why*. To me this was highly memorable.

When they are not tied to a job, there is nothing they like more than following the steelhead around the state. It seems an enviable existence, but when business is good, they work long hours. She pulls the load during those times when Moe must fish or perish. To get along with a steelheader it is necessary to make accommodations, since the steelheader is inflexible by definition. There should be a Hall of Fame for the spouses and companions of male steelheaders, and an annual award given to the one who has sacrificed the most. A person who gives up so much for another deserves to be institutionalized, and often has to be.

A couple of Moe instances: One morning I arose at my usual time and ate a leisurely breakfast. I performed my ablutions and drew on my waders, taking the time to replace a leader tippet that was slightly frayed, something I rarely bother to do. I strolled down the beach to my favorite pool. Where was Moe? He was resting under the recently picked d'Anjous trees, up on the bank. He had fished the pool steadily throughout the morning, with what success I did not know. He saw me coming and hurried down the bank and into the water. I went elsewhere.

That evening I returned from fishing Monitor. Moe was fishing in front of my camp. "Hi, Moe," I greeted him. He looked at me with alarm. Here he was, several yards out in the water, while I was high and dry on the path through the pear trees, where I could reach the main pool in no time. This we both knew. "Race you to the pool," I said, cheerfully. I thought it was funny as hell.

Moe leaped out of the water and began running down the beach. He was ahead of me by twenty yards when I turned away. I never thought he would take me seriously.

Nothing Moe loves more than to catch a string of steelhead on a weekend while I'm back in Seattle. Rather than let me guess about his success, he insists on relating it to me, strike by strike, fish by fish, run by run, until I am inclined to run myself. The numbers are often astronomical. I believe him.

He has the uncanny knack of timing his arrival at a pool at the same time as the fish. Newly arrived steelhead are usually avid takers. Moe will stand at the head of a run without moving his feet, catching fish after fish, until the river runs out of steelhead or it gets too dark for them to see his favorite black fly.

He will not get sated or quit, for he knows there is a long winter ahead and, like the ant, he wants to store up food on which to feed. His "food" is memories and events with which to astound and confuse his friends. Soul food, you might say.

To say that Moe is a good fisher, an excellent fisher, is to say the obvious. But there is something about so fine a fisher that is wearisome, heedless. He brings you down, or, rather, he brings *me* down.

If you like to compete, Moe is there for you to compete with. If you don't like to compete, Moe is still there.

Moe is a natural force, almost a force of nature. He is as prevailing as the wind. I have seen him tired, out on his feet, but never discouraged, never defeated. For a steelheader of his ilk, there is always tomorrow, for isn't a terrible day often followed by a great one?

It is, in the fall, on the Wenatchee. Others persist or luck out and do well, too. One night on the Wenatchee, I got a fish and Stan Young didn't. The next day he hooked six or eight and landed six or eight. Numbers become vague and a little unreal, after a certain point on an exceptional day.

That night Stan yawned. The fishing was too easy on the Wenatchee, he said. He was packing up his tent trailer at the county park and moving in the morning to the Methow. Maybe things there would be more difficult, more rewarding.

I stayed and I persisted. Then I moved off to the Ronde. I stayed and I tried there. I didn't do well. I returned to the Wenatchee and it welcomed me with fish. (Blessèd river.)

Moe was there. He was scoring, too. He caught more fish than I did, he often does. At dusk we often sought the same pool at Monitor. I like to have it to myself. So I left it to him evenings and came back mornings about eleven o'clock, when I could be alone. He was elsewhere, perhaps working, which he is known to do. Usually I got one fish, sometimes I hooked two. Rarely I hooked three, landing two. Evenings Moe knocked them dead. He had his usual multiple fish evenings. It was like catching trout.

"This is nothing but glorified trout fishing," Bill Nelson had told Dub Price, on a different river. I agree.

One year—like a hardy perennial—Moe wintered over. He found work in Wenatchee and when he could shake free he drove out along the river road over newly fallen snow and old ice. He walked down to a favorite shrunken hole and gave the dark water a few casts. The steelhead were there and, though loggy, would sometimes strike. He had good fishing. There was next to no competition. Once or twice he saw a man's tracks in the snow, heading out to a good pool, but never the man. Then, near the season's end, he met him. It was another fly fisher, a man I don't know. Both had had good fishing for the full winter.

True, the fish were dark and sluggish, but they were unspawned steelhead at a certain fixed point in their life cycle. They were killing time, waiting until the water warmed, the daylight hours grew longer, and their spawn fully developed to the point where it drove them up onto the redds. This would be in spring, a time of turbulent water, when it was next to impossible to fish for them. In a slowed and reduced river, winter brought almost summer-like conditions, or even worse because of the ice, and the steelhead were restricted in their choices of lies. It was easy to determine where in a run they might be and to fish right on top of them. It was a cold winter, and fishing times often turned out to be when there was a thaw for an hour or so in the day and the sun (such as it was) stood directly overhead. Then the line would not freeze in the guides and more than the initial cast could be made before icing up.

You have to be a diehard fly fisher (one with antifreeze in your veins) to go out after steelhead in the bitter cold. Moe was one. Of course he used sinking lines, but there are winter times when a floating line will continue to catch fish. The season calls for flies that are tied on heavy irons (such as 6X strong) or else have their shanks weighted with lead fuse wire before the body is wrapped on.

It is much like spring trout fishing with weighted nymphs. In fact, our winter fly techniques were lifted from this type of fishing. The fly is cast upstream, almost like a dry, and coils of line gathered back in as the fly sinks and comes toward you, for the line is to be played out again in a series of mends as it passes you and continues on its course. Often the fly will be felt striking bottom; this is important information and tells you how to fish out the rest of the drift, for you don't want to hang up in the rocks and lose the fly; at the same time as you want to continue fishing deep, for the steelhead will not move much for your fly and you want to hit the fish right on the nose.

So there are only surface similarities to summer dry-line fishing. Somebody as determined to fish this way as Bill McMillan, and his growing army of followers (Moe is one), make the steelhead take the fly presented this way. Others switch to conventional sunk-fly techniques. I am among their numbers.

THIRTY-SEVEN

In September, winter still seems a long ways off (though it is not), the days as hot as ever, the river shrunken, the nights not yet cool. If you like warm weather, summer is for you. It is not for me. I look forward to crisp nights and days when the temperature doesn't get past 70 degrees. When that nippy time comes, winter is pressing. Its effects will be felt in a week or two.

I owe Tom Crawford a huge debt for his beneficence. He first told me about the White Creek water on the Sauk, where for a number of years I did very well, up until the Great Flood of 1990, when the best part of that hole disappeared. Tom also told me about what I now call the Camp Pool on the Wenatchee. Every October he comes over and overnights with me and gives me a continuing lesson on how to catch steelhead. This I am not particularly grateful for, but since Tom is good company the annual lesson is worth the price.

I try to keep him up late, talking. It is not hard to do. In return, he is supposed to sleep in in the morning and not get a jump on the good water while I stay in the sack. This is impossible to do; he doesn't need sleep. As a former triathlete his energy level doesn't deplete throughout the day. My own starts out at low level and goes downhill from there.

Of course I have twenty years on Tom. I wish he would acknowledge it and give me a concession. No, I don't. When he does, I will know my days of effectiveness are over and he is humoring an old fart who is no longer a player in the game.

So he promotes a jovial competition—and generally wins. You'd think he'd get tired of out-fishing me, wouldn't you? (Who ever gets tired of winning?)

One fall Tom came back from the Skeena. He'd had great luck on a floating line and could see no reason to switch over to a sink tip, just because he was back in the USA. Steelhead were steelhead, weren't they? They were international in character; there was no basic difference between a steelhead from, say, the Bulkley or the Morice, or even the Kispiox, and one headed for the Wenatchee, Methow, or Grande Ronde. Since he was a fish biologist, he no doubt was aware that the races of steelhead in eastern Washington were closer to the Skeena fish than to the ones from our Skykomish or Stillaguamish systems. This meant they had an inherent interest in what was happening on or near the surface.

The on-or-near element is important. Tom for the most part fished a fly designed to sink. It was tied on what is called an ordinary salmon hook, that is, one that is twice as stout as some mythical standard hook. It was called 1X strong. Now dry-fly hooks used for steelhead and Atlantic salmon are generally Wilsons and are 2X light or fine, and they are usually 1X long, which means their shank is the length of the next size larger hook. Thus, a Wilson 6 will be as long as a low-water 4, but the wire will be much finer. Its gape is big, too, as big as an ordinary salmon hook size two, but it is light and fine, designed to help a fly float. Its short point is very sharp. It doesn't have to be struck hard to sink in up to its tiny barb and catch.

A Wilson (it is made by Partridge, in Reddich, England) is flat-forged and will not straighten out, not unless the pull comes from right angles to the point of the hook, which is unlikely when playing a fish. It might snap before it straightens out. On small hooks anglers have a choice between which gives first. A hook under the wrong kind of stress will either break, generally at the barb, or it will straighten out. Most of us prefer one that will break. If we stick with one manufacturer, we get to know a hook's strengths and weaknesses. We may occasionally break a hook off while banging it on the rocks behind us. This is more likely than breaking it on a fish.

A hook that straightens out under right-angled pressure is an abomination; one never knows just how much pull it will take to cause it to gape. Now there are frequent times when you have to pull hard against a steelhead. To know that your hook will not straighten out offers constant reassurance. To put it another way, not knowing when your hook may gape will cause you to play your fish unduly lightly because you are afraid for your hook, and this is intolerable.

Tom, in this instance, used good, stout hooks. They would never gape and would break only when hit repeatedly with a hammer, or if hit too hard on a rock. (We all bang our hooks on stones because we are trying for the longest possible cast, most of the time, and to do this we risk a low backcast, and there are generally rocks behind us.) Such a hook is heavy enough to sink in all but the swiftest water. There was no very swift water around.

It is impossible to dress an ordinary salmon hook to float for more than a few feet on its initial cast. From then on, false cast as you may, it immediately assumes a rapidly sinking configuration. This is a fancy way of saying it will sink like a stone. It will not be content to remain in Frank Amato's definitive one inch of the surface. More likely it will sink at a fixed rate until it is clanging along the bottom.

This is not exactly dry-fly fishing. Nor is it greased-line fishing, which is intended to keep the fly awash in the surface film—or about half an inch beneath it. It is something else. It is wet-fly fishing, but with a line that floats. So what's the matter with that? Not a thing. It is effective. When a fish takes, though, it is with a wet-fly strike, and most often it will not be observed, for the fly is riding deep.

What's wrong with that?

Nothing, nothing. But let's not pretend it is something that it isn't. It is wet-fly fishing with a dry line, and it is a good way of getting steelhead to hit under low and mid-water conditions. It will even produce strikes during moderately high water conditions.

I resort to it often—more likely on the east side than on the west, however. The main purpose is to get the fly down, but keep it out of the rocks. This requires a subtle balance. With a long leader on a full-floating line, I can come up to the surface with a simple change of fly, and nothing else, or I can tie on a sparse low-water dressing and fish just under the surface, which is a telling place.

The Partridge low-water hooks that anglers have fished with for decades can be made to behave quite differently, depending on their size and (again) on the wire gauge used in their manufacture. The big ones sink really fast. One might forget that A.H.E. Wood used what he called "large irons" during the spring run-off. Most were ordinary salmon hooks; he used them in sizes up to 4/0. He only resorted to his famed low-water series (including the painted bare hooks called Red Shanks and Blue Shanks) in times of greatly reduced flows. Low-water fly design demands a slender, sleek body and a wing that is lightly dressed. Aside from its aerodynamic shape that is so attractive to anglers, it has the merit of offering little resistance to penetrating the surface film and quickly sinking to some depth. Often this is considerable.

If you don't believe me, try this experiment. First tie on a number two fully dressed fly on an ordinary salmon hook. Soak it good and make sure the leader point is the same in the both instances. Let's say it is my standard eight-pound test. At the edge of the seam, let the wetted fly sink on a slack leader and record the time it takes to reach a depth, let us say, of three feet.

Now tie on a 1/0 low-water Partridge that is sparsely dressed and has a tiny head of the kind Syd Glasso originated, or try an Alec Jackson Spey hook, which is about the same gauge size but even stronger. Wetted ahead of time or not (*not* is just as good for my purposes), drop the fly on the surface of the same eddy. Immediately the low-water hook enters the water with no resistance from the eye or materials in the surface film. So already it is ahead of the other fly in beginning to fish effectively. Now watch the fly, watch it sink. It descends (bend first, to be sure, in such slack) remarkably fast. Soon

Syd Glasso

it is below the three-foot visibility level of the river and out of sight. Unmistakably it is on the bottom in such slow water.

Now try it again with the low-water fly, but out in the seam more, further out at the edge of the current. The leader holds the fly's head up, the hook riding along in the quickened water in the proper stance—streaming with the current, as if riding on it. When such a current is available, which is after the river has come back up in the fall, a low-water-designed fly comes into its own and fishes well, but up until then, the current is so slack, the moving channel and seam so narrow, a fly like my Spade—with its supportive tail and ability to present the same shape, silhouette, and arrangement of elements time after time, however much it twists and turns on the leader—is superior; you only have to fish first one and then the other to see why and how.

The next year Tom began the season with a ten-foot sink tip. I didn't ask why the switch, but I knew he was again newly returned from British Columbia, and perhaps it was what was working there this year. His fly was the same as I saw him using before. It is called Bush Baby and I should pass along the dressing because it is a good one and I have caught many steelhead on it. (See Fly Plate Number 7.)

The tail is gray squirrel, medium long. The body black chenille, ribbed with oval silver tinsel. (Flat tinsel is just as good.) The wing is more gray squirrel, tied so that the bars of black and silver line up with the tail's bars; this makes the wing fairly long, but not so long as to twist and wrap around the bend of the hook. The hackle—I'll bet you guessed it, since this is rapidly becoming one of the famous black flies—is soft grizzly, and Tom ties it Cosseboom style, the way I like to tie many of my own flies, so it goes on last and is slanted nicely backwards by doubling.

In the wing he will often lay on some pearlescent Flashabou. I tie it both ways, but prefer it without. The hook is a two or a four, ordinary salmon. With chenille and squirrel as its essential elements, the fly will not float, even if you whip it back and forth in the air. Where does it fish? It depends on the length of your leader, how much (if any) of the line itself sinks, and the speed of the current.

At the top of Merlin's Pool, for instance, at dead-low water, Bush Baby tied Tom's way and fished on a floating line can be made to hang up in the rocks in the first third of the run, depending on when and how you throw your mends. Another third of the way down the pool, the fly will sink to between six inches and three feet, I'd say. (I'd have to don a wet suit and follow it through its drift to know for sure.) At the bottom third of the pool, the fly on a nine-foot leader will probably sink four to six feet. The bottom isn't much deeper than this, only a foot or two more, and when the water slows further the fly can't help but continue its downward course. Yet it rarely meets the rocks in such a manner as to catch there and lodge.

You call this dry-fly fishing? No, I never did. All I said was it is conducted with a floating line. It is wet-fly fishing, without a doubt. Why do people call it dry-fly fishing, then? Because they want to mislead you. Dry-fly fishing is an elitist activity and to have caught your fish on a "floating" fly is supposed to be superior sport. They believe they deserve more credit for having gotten their fish to take on the surface. If you want to believe this, go ahead. As Tom Smothers says, "Some people believe chickens have lips."

In other words, believe what you will, but you are better off fishing the floating line while the water and air are warm. With a line that floats you can fish a wide variety of ways—from the true top to right on down to the firm bottom. The people above and below you in a run won't know the difference, not unless they are watching the surface for signs of disturbance from your fly which, of course, they won't be able to see. If they ask you where your fly is, you can always say it has drowned.

On top is good often enough that it shouldn't be forsaken. Keep your fly right on the surface, most of the time. It is a pleasant place to be, for it is fully visible to you and your fishing neighbor. When you hook the fish that you are apt to, your whistle of astonishment will not be the only one to fill the air.

THIRTY-EIGHT

R oderick Haig-Brown said it first, like many things, and like many things he said it best. It is more fun to fish on top, and if you don't believe it is effective, you can always go through the water wet afterwards. I often do.

He used to fish upstream, always putting his classically floated fly over fish that hadn't seen it before. This is textbook trout-fisher's stuff. Drag is to be avoided, the fly is kept floating intentionally, and the line is rapidly gathered into coils as the fly comes barrelling downstream at you after each cast. A taking fish is a big surprise (though you are always expecting one) and you find yourself with a hand full of slack line and a fish trying to take the coils away faster than you can release them. It is surprising that you don't lose more fish this way than you do. There must be a minor god whose duty it is to watch over upstream, dry-fly fishers and protect them from ordinary mishaps.

This is quick, exciting fishing, but when the steelhead are not responsive, or when the juvenile activity is so great that you fear for the mortality you might be causing, you may wish to fish some other way. Also, it is tiring. Long rod or short, the number of false casts necessary to dry off the fly, and the rapidity with which they must be executed, often unstarches a fisher long before he'd like to quit this form of torture. His wrist aches, his shoulder, too, and his eyes are gritty from staring so long into the sun, trying to spot his small fly.

I've actually begun to see double after a few hours of this. It is why I often resort to fishing dry "blind." It makes for an unavoidably slow strike, and this is just the right thing to do. *Trying* to do it while the fly is visible is not humanly possible and the eager strike doesn't result in a hookup, most times; you usually either take the fly away from the fish that isn't quite there yet, or you break the fly off in its mouth, which is worse, believe me.

Fishing blind, often into the sun, forcing yourself to be inattentive, is fun and productive. The fly floats as best it can, according to the kind of water it finds itself in, how it was tied, its materials, and how much and how recently you've greased it.

If you can't see it, or can't see it *well,* you may not care too precisely how it is fishing, and that may be all for the best. The fish will come to it whatever way it can, if it chooses to.

With a few twists of the fingers, you can switch to fishing wet and the big wet fly you select can be made to fish deep, in traditional wet-fly fashion, tried and true, or it can be made to behave like crazy by the addition of a couple of riffling hitches. Such a hitch applied to a fly like a Muddler Minnow or various greased liners, with riffling ruffs built in, is a case of overkill. The hitch shouldn't be necessary and these flies don't require it, so it should be saved for flies that are intended to sink or are ordinarily dressed. Thus, riffling offers a wonderful change-of-pace tactic for a marabou or a slant-winged wet fly.

You can be sure not a fish in the shrunken pool will miss seeing it. They will notice it in exactly same manner as we view a tiny motorboat set loose in a child's wading pond. How can such a commotion be ignored?

If you continue to fish on top, you will eventually be rewarded with a visible strike, often several of them. Sometimes the multiple strikes all occur in the same cast or drift; this is frustrating and confusing. Jock Scott says the salmon is "missing the fly." (I suspect Arthur Wood would not echo this sentiment, but would say the fish is playing with the angler and the fly, and may or may not take it later, even further along in the same cast or drift.)

Best have a strong heart and nerves of steel. Superman is the ideal candidate for the job, but can he pass the physical? (By the way, did Lee Wulff ever tremble with excitement? Did he ever shake so, before or after a fish, that he had trouble threading his leader through the eye of the next fly? I suspect he did, and how I would love to have had that confirmed.)

Is a surface take really that bad? No, it is that *good.* Surface takes are breathtaking, and that is why we seek them. They are astonishingly swift. They are violent. The fish that has been content to lie quietly in its riffle suddenly goes berserk—and it is not because of the sting of the barb of the hook. The mayhem occurs *before* the barb is felt, or can be thought to be felt. The result is instant mayhem. The fish literally flings itself at the fly, coming out of the water to do it and throwing caution to the wind.

Why? Beats me, but I know that it happens, and that is all you need to know on earth, and all that matters, too.

You stand hip-deep or a little shallower at the head of a riffle like Merlin's Pool and cast a surface fly across the water and let it swing of its own accord across the run that breaks slightly away from you. You make a mend or two to help the fly move along its course, to aid it, if you possibly can, and the fish . . . explodes.

A wet-fly take in such shallow water often produces something similar. But it is different, too. It is milder. The fish is not apt to go into the air until stung and restraint is applied. The surface-taking fish explodes upon the moment of taking the fly; there is no pause, no hesitation, no spare second in which the angler can count his fingers and make sure they are all present and accounted for and able to function. The strike is quick. It has a violence the sunk-fly take lacks. The fish quickly acquires speed in racing across the pool—or up or down it—that seems faster than a wet-fly fish.

Perhaps the floating line retards the fish's movement less, enabling it to break away faster. That's it. It is a sprint, not a race, but that doesn't mean it is over with sooner. Quite the contrary. With such speed, the sprinting fish is likely to cover more distance and do it faster. You are left wondering how the fish got from here to there so quickly, the line trailing pathetically slowly after it and only eventually catching up. You shake your head in awe and disbelief. It has just happened to you. Wonderful! What is more, the fish did not break your tippet, with all its power and speed. You are still attached by gossamer and now every time your fish moves off, you watch the colorful floating line give chase across the tranquil river, striving to catch up. Why, you can even *offer* your fish line as a tactic, laying out a coil or two on the surface to protect against breakage as you back up towards the beach where you will eventually land the fish—if only it slows down a little and turns ultimately on its side.

Which seems unlikely now, at the start of the battle.

THIRTY-NINE

Each year I say to myself, "It is time to go back to the Ronde." It is September, the month progressing, and I have kept half a weather eye cocked on the information that is printed in the back of the sports pages about the numbers of salmon and steelhead counted daily over each of the dams on the Columbia and Snake. Ice Harbor is a critical one and the numbers of steelhead tabulated each day are soon in the thousands. It would take but a tiny fraction of one percent to satisfy me. Is that too much to ask of the river gods?

At the same time I am suspicious of all fish numbers. Thousands? I could believe hundreds, maybe. If the count was twenty or thirty steelhead a day, it might be more in the realm of plausibility.

"How many fish did you catch on the Ronde last year?" somebody might ask an angler. "Two thousand," he might jokingly reply. "That's a lot." "Well, there were a lot of them. Just look at the dam counts published in the paper."

The Ronde is so beautiful, it will not stay long out of my mind, with its deep, shadowy recesses and broad, glinting riffles. There remains the pull of personalities and river reaches—old friends, old rivalries, old triumphs, old failures needing to be overcome. The competitive element is strong.

Each year lately the Ronde calls, but I don't go back. I've sorted out two reasons. First is the crowds. I've seen bad days on the Wenatchee, but never like an average October day on the lower Ronde. Such a day on the Wenatchee will blow over; just wait for tomorrow. The river returns to its normal, sparsely populated self. On the Wenatchee there are some fair pools (they'd be outstanding anywhere else) that don't get fished in a day. Some don't get fished in a week. On the Ronde it is rare for a pool to be deserted for more than an hour or two. There is a gang of avid steelheaders overnighting in the two or three makeshift campgrounds and they are in general agreement on what is important. They behave alike. They go to bed right after supper, often while the sun still colors the sky, and the campgrounds look like graveyards for old RVs.

The happenstance campgrounds are clotted with their campers, small trailers, and great-masted motor schooners. They look like a carnival forming, or a circus ready to break apart. I exaggerate, of course, but not by much. You have to see it to believe it.

You can bet these dudes will all be fumbling around in the dark a few hours hence, rustling up a quicky breakfast and not having their big meal until ten or eleven o'clock, when they come in dog-tired and ravenous, ready for steak and eggs or griddle cakes.

Each morning these guys cheerfully race each other to and through their favorite pools, which number eight or ten. Take twenty guys and ten pools and perform some simple long division and you come up with two guys to a pool at any given time, and since not all of those pools are absolutely first-rate, you will have three or four men on some pools, one on the others, most of the time. No, thanks. You can have it.

Then there are the hunters. It used to be a sportsman's hat trick to go to the Ronde in October and pack out two steelhead, a buck, and a limit of chukars. It is still possible (for hatchery steelhead can be kept at the mouth section now), and there are those who find satisfaction in killing their limits. Anything short of a game limit represents failure to them, and anybody who doesn't agree is showing his lack of prowess, his unmanliness.

And there is the noise element. Many times each morning there comes the sound of a high-powered rifle rattling down the canyon walls and reverberating into loud silence. Did a man just get his deer? No, no, they're just sighting in their rifles. I've seen men in a hunters' camp banging away with deer rifles at some natural scenic target on the other side of the river until a box of ammo lay empty. About fifty pointless shots were fired off in stupid succession. Apparently "sightings in" have to be performed frequently and don't hold true for long, and some men love to hear the crack of a round. (I heard enough in the Army to last a lifetime.) With all the rifle noise a deer would have to be stone deaf not to go elsewhere. Maybe all the deer that get killed have lost their hearing and this accounts for their demise.

So I will be content to dream of the Ronde, and its majestic beauty, but will do my fishing elsewhere—unless I am feeling unusually competitive and aggressive. I hope not to be. I would much rather take my time on the tranquil and bucolic Wenatchee, thank you.

FORTY

J ust as there is a time when a river goes over to surface fishing, there comes a time when it goes back to fish taking near the bottom. All summer long you know it is coming and, in a way, dread it, though you love wet-fly fishing and feel it is what you do best.

You keep fishing on top, believing in it, at least in principle, loving the excitement of the surface take and asking the minor gods who preside over such fish and fishing for one more good day. And sometimes you get one.

Temperature is the important ingredient in the steelhead fly-fishing recipe. The river in October starts out with a daytime temperature near 70 degrees. I can't stop my dog Sam from entering a pool and wading right up to his white chin, I don't blame him any. After a hot day, I will strip to my Jockeys and walk down the sandy bank to the riffle in front of my camp and wade right up to my human chin. I have been known to soap up and wash my hair, the water being warm enough still to rinse away the suds and leave me feeling clean.

Soon the nights grow cool and I can pull my sleeping bag up around my ears and sleep deeply, comfortably, not twisting and turning throughout the night, or awakening in a lather. Nor do I hear the east-bound freights in the middle of the night (or rather hear them only on a subliminal level). The river remains low and the noise-level from Highway 2 is high; it takes a tall river to drown out the traffic. Mornings are nippy and the shock of the river on my legs in their thin, plastic waders comes as a pleasant surprise. I don light-weight wool pants for the mornings now. When I remember to plunge my thermometer in the current for the requisite slow count to fifteen, it comes back with a reading in the high fifties. By afternoon the extra pants are shed and I know without measurement the water temperature is back in the sixties. The air never exceeds the high sixties now.

When I take a dip to cool or clean off, there is a fierce shock. I think that I am getting old and unable to take much change. My thermometer tells me it is more likely that a sixty-plus degree bathtub is not for most people and I notice the soap doesn't exactly wash off; I actually have to towel it away and my skin feels a bit slick afterwards. I think I have taken my last outdoor bath for the year.

It is the end of the first week in October and the county park is shutting down; the RV people seek warmth and are heading south. Moe and I can no longer use the quarter showers at the park. We've acquired an aroma much like my dog, Sam. The red delicious hang from the tree much as they have for weeks, thick as cherries, but still they are not ready for picking. I can eat my fill and more from what has fallen early to the ground. Overhead an ear-splitting helicopter sprays No Drop. The pilot sees me fishing and I wave; he waggles what passes for wings.

Last year Larry Peterson lost a friend when the man's copter crashed in an orchard. People say he might have hit a wire, but, hell, he knew where all the wires were. People say that copter pilots, and those that fly light planes for dusting, don't plan on living long. It is one reason why they make the good money that they do. Larry also says it isn't all that much, but they just love to fly; maybe it is why they live such crazy lives. They want to store up memories for the darkness that follows.

I've eaten so many windfall apples that I have red cheeks. Also, I've been invited to cart home as many as I'd like—to eat, to give to friends for immediate consumption, or to make into sauce. I've noticed that all my old trails to the river that were lined last year with that pretty bright shrub, poison ivy, are rid of it. I attribute it to the hatchery fish I gave to the various orchard owners. When they sprayed Round Up in the spring, they thought of me and my path down to the river, remembering how badly I break out in a rash. So those fish I killed for them had some additional benefit? Good.

In the morning, where the grass between the fruit trees is packed hard, there is frost, and it shines like silver threads when the sun breaks over the golden hills. In fact, the air is so bright that I have to shield my eyes with my hand for a moment or go briefly blind. When I say, "Whoo," to the day, it looks as though I'm smoking, I say it several times, just to watch my words form and disperse.

Sam sleeps in a ball and is slow to uncoil. Immediately he goes in search of a sunny spot. I find it hard to climb out of my sleeping bag and bury myself deeper an extra fifteen minutes, dozing. I resist the urge to turn on the space heater; instead, after finishing my breakfast, I manfully sit in the watery sun with my coffee cup trembling, and notice that the air is scarcely warmer than inside my trailer.

Larry tells me the temperature hit thirty. He knows these things the way an old Indian does, I recognize that he is right, because my wading shoes from last night are lightly frozen. My first morning duty is to place them in the sun so they will be soft enough to jam on my feet, an hour hence.

The river is up a little, for the Icicle River diversion has ended and also the Peshastin one. Those along the Main Line are being shut off, one by one, but there are many to go. I see the rocks on the far side of the Camp Pool exposing a little less of themselves and the river sliding faster over the gut out in front. The back eddy is smaller, and I am thankful for the change. When I enter the water the cold grabs me. I brace for the shock. Sam stays up on the stones, with only his fleshless ankles wet. His legs are pure bone, all the way up.

River life has responded to the drop in temperature. I feel whitefish banging on my fly throughout its drift and ultimately I hook one. It is shiny and odd-looking—a salmonid, true, yet not much like the others. It is hooked in the mouth that forms an O. The river is richer for having the family of whitefish in it. I believe it is all the richer for the suckers and squawfish, too, though don't ask me to explain with precision their functioning in the complex ecosystem. I simply believe that they belong there and contribute to the river's bright diversity and health.

Chinooks are spawning and occasionally stick their broad black backs out of the center of the river near or just to the slack side of the seam. I have mixed feelings about hooking them and am curious until after I have played the first one, after which I would just as soon not have another encounter until next year. Hooked in the mouth, I can usually manage to land one on eight-pound test Maxima, given enough time, but who wants to waste forty minutes on an innocent fish that only wishes to spawn and get its life over with? I know I should not test myself, my prowess, on salmon, and usually do not, but the challenge remains each year until I fair hook one. Then I am sorry.

There are steelhead arriving in increasing numbers, as the peak of the season approaches, then passes. I'd like to say they were bright, but they aren't, and it is hard to make a case for more than the relative brightness of some females that are prettily colored like a lake rainbow trout. The males—some of them quite big—look to be in full spawning dress, but I know they are not. It is an illusion, their ripeness months away.

The steelhead is why I am here. It always is.

FORTY-ONE

It is a cool morning, after a cold night, and I must thaw out my wading shoes with the space heater, for I forgot to bring them inside last night and must pay the price. This delays my morning fishing for another ten or fifteen minutes. Finally, annoyed at the wait, I draw them on with great difficulty, half-thawed. They yield to the pressure and my feet feel the strain, once I have forced them on. I also don wading cleats, for the stones remain slick. They won't be scrubbed clean until sustained high water. This morning I refuse to carry a staff (though I have a folding one secreted in my big back pocket, along with a lightweight rain jacket, just in case).

Somewhat perversely I choose to fish again on top. There is something about the floating line sailing so sweetly through the air that makes me loath to give it up. I am hooking (and usually landing) about a fish a day; if not one on a given day, then two the next, or the day after that. I am fishing about six hours. That's all that is fun for me, and any more begins to resemble manual labor.

There are quite a few fish in the river, and I suspect I would do better fishing deep. But doggedly I stick to the floater.

The Camp Pool has come up enough to have a straightforward, even flow again, and is a joy to fish. If nobody has been through it by the time I am ready, I will start there with high expectations. I am wearing ultralight waders because they do not bog me down, but I am wearing heavy wool

The author.

pants underneath and a down jacket on top, which I know I will have to peel off in an hour or so.

The water is a shock, but I love it: I take cold well. It is delightful because a river ought to run cold, and recently the Wenatchee has been so warm that I am alarmed about the health of its fish and their survival. I play a daily game with the river. I try to guess its temperature. I'd say forty-eight degrees. Usually in plastic waders I'm never off by more than two degrees. Then I reconsider my initial guess and thoughtfully fine-tune it. I want to come closer than two degrees—I want to hit it right on the button. About the time I leave the first pool I make myself stop for a thermometer plunge that will verify or disprove my guess. It takes fifteen long seconds. Forty-eight it is. I win today's prize, whatever it is.

I waste no time. Each cast is thoroughly fished-out, then carefully repeated, but not in exactly the same way or place. It goes either a shade more upstream or down, and my mends are different, too, either bigger or smaller. Each part of the pool plumbs my memory for past takes in exactly the same spots; even though I can consciously recall only a few of them, the rest of them nag at me dimly. I try to repeat the former cast and recall the take that followed as best my hands and eyes remember it, but the only strike I have in the first third of the pool is from a hungry squawfish, one of about three pounds that does a good steelhead imitation for about fifteen seconds before it gets levered up on top and examined to determine its species. Then I horse it in and shake it loose from my fingertips, knowing there are no forward teeth to worry about.

There is something about a squawfish's take on top that gives you assurance all the river species still have something left of a surface orientation. With some flies, such as my Spade, the fly only has to be drifting along naturally in the current to engender a soft, serious strike or peck. Other brighter flies draw a scrapfish strike only when they are stripped in, I've noticed, so I stick with the Spade, at least for a while. It is a confidence builder.

The pool gives me no more action and I am tempted to fish it wet, but don't; instead I return to camp and car and drive off in the direction of Monitor, stopping long enough to buy the Seattle morning paper, to which I am addicted. It now costs seventy-five cents here, a rip-off, but I need my fix—news from the outside world.

In Merlin's Pool, I hook a nice fish halfway down, but lose it after the first, long run. I pound the pool repeatedly for the next hour-and-a-half but am able to raise no more steelhead, though I take a nice jack Chinook, one that has residualized and looks and behaves much like a rainbow trout. Catching juveniles, even so late in the season, and with the water growing colder daily, is no test of either my prowess or the effectiveness of fishing a certain way, I know, for these fish are doing the last of the feeding that will carry them through the winter. The real test is an adult steelhead. (Isn't it always?)

I read and write and visit with friends throughout the long afternoon. Though the sun is shining, I feel the need of a light coat over my shirt that is partly wool. Just before dark, I make a pass through the Camp Pool, but have no touch to a bright surface fly. Lately mornings have been productive, with nights uneventful. Most autumns are like this, at least for me. But I still fish for exceptions.

It is really cold tonight, reaching what I guess to be freezing long before midnight. I go to bed earlier than usual, for the sake of warmth, and take a book with me. A heavy wool blanket is unfurled alongside me, just in case; I discover by morning that I've pulled it up over me sometime during the night. The newly-risen river masks the roar of the highway traffic and the rumble of the night's long freight train, for which I am grateful. I've slept well, am thoroughly rested.

My boots are warm and dry, due to the lesson learned yesterday. Each year about this time I have to be taught it again. I've brought them inside. Wet boots . . . freeze, so early in the year? You'd better believe it.

My rod is left strung up with last night's fly on the top of the trailer, about seven feet off the ground; I have to stand on tiptoe to reach it. I put it there butt-first, so the prevailing wind will not blow it off. The wind today is steady but not strong so far. The sky is thinly clouded, the sun discernible as a lemon wedge over humped-backed hills the color of caramel.

This morning's squawfish takes on the strip and does a brief steelhead imitation. The water *feels* colder. I'd guess it to be two degrees lower, but will have to wait until I quit the pool in an hour for confirmation with my thermometer. For now I just want to fish.

A fish takes near the bottom of the pool but immediately comes off. I would like to say, "Steelhead," but can't for sure. It had good heft in the current, though.

I go to Merlin's Pool, but touch nothing. Then I drive to the county park, which is often good for a fish at this time of year, with the water up, the temperature down. It seems peculiar—almost like trespassing—to wander at will through its ghostly golf course-like setting, all the motor homes and long, luxury-class trailers vanquished. The caretaker on duty knows me and gives me a cheerful wave; a week ago, I negotiated trespass permission.

The pool is long, slow, and boring, but it is often full of fish. It is so long that to fish it the way I like would take me six solid hours, so I enter it low and fish only a critical portion, a section I've come to find dependable at this or most any height. One half-hearted pull results and nothing else.

I walk back to my vehicle over a carpet of golden aspen and cottonwood leaves. The trees are mostly bare, the sky greatly opened up. As always it is blue, without a wisp of white to mar its smoothness. I stop in town for some groceries. Through the long afternoon I read a Graham Greene "entertainment"—which written by anybody else would be a major novel.

Instead of fishing the Camp Pool tonight, I decide to eat at the Trading Post Tavern, which serves jumbo burgers. This may be my last night of the season, for I have serious reservations about staying, with the weather getting worse by the day. I dread a blizzard at Stevens Pass. The night is going to be cold, and with daylight saving's time newly ended, the hours of darkness begin at five. I watch a football game at the sports bar and linger over my giant schooner. Then I return to camp, bundle up well, and read into the night, but I soon end up in the sack for warmth. Sam is holed up in a small cavern he has hollowed out in the sand like some wild creature. Overhead the black sky sparkles. The frost is down by nine.

In the night I think I hear the spatter of rain on my canvas. Then silence. I awaken to a great whiteness, glistening. It has snowed thinly. The rain I heard turned to snow and muffled the living world. The snow is a fine, powdery stuff. It will take a lot more to make up an inch. The wind has quickened and blows the light dust scudding across the paved apron where, a month ago, the fruit trucks collected bins of Lawrence's pears and—in the heat and dust—brought them to their new home in the controlled-atmosphere warehouse.

I climb into my layers and prepare breakfast. As my coffee water heats, I amuse myself by blowing my breath into the air and watching it form cumulus. There is something positively gruesome about pouring hot coffee into a frigid human body—it makes me colder. I hurry into my fishing togs and, because of the bite of the wind, pull my rain parka over my down jacket. Now I've got on about everything I brought with me for autumn.

I choose to fish on top again, foolishly determined. At the heart of the pool—right out from the marker rocks, which are all underwater now—I fling out cast after cast, demanding a steelhead to come up and hit my fly. I *know* they are there. They just have to be; it is nearly November. But not a bump.

I have trouble getting the line to go back and forth through my guides. Why? Ice crystals have formed there. Should I switch to a sinking line and wet fly? Sure, I should, but I'm not going to, not yet. Instead I drive to Merlin's Pool and continue my surface fishing. The sky has clouded over and is a peculiar shade of gray. From above a fine light powder is falling. It is nothing to worry about yet.

I've stuck it out a week longer than I intended to. Lawrence—Larry's dad—tells me that there is never snow that lasts until Thanksgiving, and though I do not doubt him I remain uneasy. What is coming down from above is not rain, and it is coating the ground. The wind picks up, swirling the flakes overhead and making them whirl. I cast my bright little fly into the upstream breeze and pray for a take. Give me a fish, O Lord. These are the words of the desperate. I lengthen out my cast—as if distance will increase my chances of getting a steelhead take. Finally, down at the bottom of the pool, I wade ashore in dismay. Sam looks up at me, questioningly, as I hesitate on the strand. Am I'm done, or aren't I? I see the snow flecking his muzzle and note how it makes him pinch his eyes.

Leave or not, he asks me? Not, I think. I am going to go through the pool one more time—*wet*.

I screw on a reel with a twenty-foot fast-sinking tip looped to the back end of a floater. That is going to get down fast. Better to go the full distance with the devil than meet him half-way. (What is this weird, religious tone that is filling my mind? Perhaps I've watched, "A River Runs Through It" one too many times.)

I go back into the pool, but enter a little lower down, for I remember how shallow the top part is and how easily I can hang up this line. I begin just opposite the cement slab that used to be part of the highway, my marker, which is entirely underwater now; I know where it is, though, by the slick formed below it. I cast to it, and find the distance longer than I remember—well, the river is up and this line doesn't kite out so easily, but it sure gets down fast.

I have on an orange marabou, with a furnace front hackle, for it is an orange kind of day. (If the sun were out, it would call for red.) I mend and wait and am immediately into a fish. It takes with a surge and heads upstream, making one creamy jump before heading downstream. In that pause I set the hook heavily, twice. Haven't I always said I am a wet-fly fisher at heart? (Yes, but my heart is fickle.)

I fumble the backing onto the spool with ragged reeling, standing deep in the water. Then I stagger by inches towards shore, winding in fast, and follow the bank downstream until I grow opposite the fish. It is a big male, I am sure, for it fights that way. For a while we exchange give-and-take pulls, and neither is winning.

It is snowing hard. The fish does not move very fast and won't tire. It makes my job more difficult. It is not a foolish fish.

I begin to overheat inside my down coat and rain parka, but for just an instant I am the right temperature. Then I am too hot. Suddenly I am much too hot. I rip the parka zipper open and vent myself. Then I pop the fasteners to my coat, which I can do with a single hard tug, as though angry at them. There, that's better.

The fish eventually moves toward the beach and I reclaim some line. Up ahead I spot the knot where my backing joins my fly line, and it seems a significant junction, portending much, so that when the knot passes through my tiptop and is cranked back on the spool where it belongs, I feel I've accomplished something great. Of course the fish immediately takes back the line and knot, undoing me. Back and forth we go, but I know I will win—if the hook doesn't pull out or the leader part at the tippet knot.

At last the fish slides into a pocket on the beach where long ago I had targeted it. It is a male, about sixteen pounds, dark, with an adipose and unnotched dorsal. I unpin it, sliding it back into the water, which is black now, a peculiar effect produced by falling snow. I re-enter the river and re-tie the fly before making my next cast. Greed motivates me. I remember that this is water I've fished steadily with a floating line and a fly that rides high in the water for weeks now. The water is forty-three degrees; I've stopped long enough to confirm it. Maybe my fish was a fluke and I would have caught it on a second pass through the pool with a surface fly. Naw.

I commence fishing again, casting wet into the wind, which is strong, and only managing to reach half my required distance. It's a long nothing. I come to the lonesome pine, then the culvert. My fly lights only about forty feet from the far bank, I notice. This is discouraging.

The river is a different river, not one exclusively mine. It is one that requires fishing with gear to be very productive. My time is about over. There is a pull, halfway through the drift, followed by a lunge and the heavy weight of a fish. The surface of the river keeps sliding by, revealing no silvery leap, no splash. My fish grinds off downstream a good distance and stops. I set the hook. Then, not sure whether I did a good job of setting it or not, I do it again. Then a third time. The fish simply lies there and takes it.

A summer fish on a floating line would be off like a rocket. It wouldn't stand for such abuse. Now the fish moves away slowly, definitively. It is much as though it remembered a not very important errand that must be attended to before nightfall. No hurry. The fish drifts away, then recalls that time is growing short, and it must hasten. There—that's more like it.

The fight is like hooking and playing a ripe Chinook, but with one difference. The fish keeps shaking its head, or rolling up on the leader, or whatever steelhead do to produce that ragged, jiggling sensation. It is worrisome, but by feeding the fish a few feet of slack I am able to stop it, for there is nothing to pull against. The battle is long and wearying for both of us.

The snow is falling heavily. Thick stuff. I think with alarm of the mountain pass I must cross today. Yes, I've overstayed my welcome, that's for sure. It was not prudent, but then who said steelheaders had common sense?

A car along the highway disgorges a man who evidently never has seen a fisher with a bowed rod before. He gets out of the car to watch. Standing tall, his hands on his hips, I see the snow spotting his slick, dark hair. Then the fish moves and demands my full attention.

Slowly the steelhead comes in to the beach. On the short line, it begins to wallow, just out from shore. More slack is fed in order for it to settle down. The fish looks like the first, but perhaps a pound lighter, which still makes it a big fish. I crank it in and face the moment of uncertainty before, balancing delicately in the shallows on its belly, it finally topples over on its side.

The man with the snow in his hair goes back to his vehicle. He returns with a hat jammed on his head. He continues to watch, fascinated.

It is a hatchery fish and I could kill it, but I don't. Life is life, and one steelhead doesn't know it is different from any other. Besides, there is no watery reason on God's planet why a wild one should go free, and a hatchery fish be killed. We've put an arbitrary value on the one, not on the other. Think about it; both have high intrinsic value and are equally entitled to live. Each deserves our respect.

The fish settles into the water, then sinks and swims away. I look up on the high bank for the snowy observer, he gives me a thumbs-up sign. I wave back. He must be a fellow fisher. When I look again, he has gone back to his car and driven away. I can see his exhaust hanging in the air. Wise man.

A white sky swims overhead. When I leave the river, my boots and Sam's feet leave white tracks on the beach. He does a happy little dance when he sees I am not going back in the water; he longs for the dry car and the long, warm ride back to Seattle. So do I.

At the Camp Pool my trailer is too wet with snow to crank it down as I must at the end of each season, even though I've been leaving it there, all folded up on its site in the orchard, for the past half-dozen winters.

"Don't worry about it," Larry tells me—my pear-orchard host and friend. "I'll take care of it." He means he will crank it down when the weather is dry. "I might not be back," I say. "I *know* you won't be back," he says with a grin. I hesitate. "I'm worried about making it through the pass, in all this snow."

"The snow," he tells me—this resident weatherman who has been wrong about only once, a decade ago, and then not by much, "will be no worse there than it is here. You'll only have this little bit when you hit Stevens Pass." "You're sure?" I ask.

He looks at me with what I adjudge to be the pity of a man who grows pears for a living for one who does not, and thus does not understand what is important in life in fruit country, such as wind and snow and rain and sun. In short, the vagaries of weather in a region famous for its seasons changing ostentatiously four full times each year. "You will have no trouble with snow in the pass," he repeats.

And he is right.

FORTY-TWO

This is in the nature of an afterword. We live and learn—if all goes well; it is what gives the adage currency. Some time passes during the writing of a book and even more while it goes through printing production. Life continues, and each of us harvests new experiences.

I've said some harsh words about Spey rods in this book and in my previous one, *Steelhead Water*. I don't exactly recant them all, but I do many of them. Spey rods *are* long and cumbersome, at least to those of us who grew up fishing single-handed fly rods. And when you walk down a wooded trail, the damned things do get caught in the limbs behind you, especially when you come to a bend. Bends there are plenty of, and they are usually choked with brambles. Woe.

But Spey rods come lighter nowadays and—my—will they ever cast a distance. For years I used a clumsy first-generation graphite two-handed rod and awkwardly made it do for me by casting overhead with it. I was, in fact, using it the day I met Trey Combs. He later became the Spey rod's champion and learned (in part from Mike Maxwell) how to manage the rather tricky style of casting they require, which is nothing like the overhead cast of a floating line discussed in this book. Meanwhile I went on with my ragged throws. Soon I put the big rod away (I thought forever) and went back to my favorite long single-handed rod and caught my share of fish on it. (I had done so on the big one, too.) That share is never as large as one wants, by the way.

In spring on one of the wide rivers that have good-sized runs of wild steelhead left in them, I saw what a good Spey caster could do with such a rod on a river whose best runs lie maybe a hundred or more feet off. Now my maximum casting distance, waded deep, with a one-handed rod is 72 feet, under optimum conditions, without resorting to monofilament shooting line, which is an abomination and comes just short of being spinning tackle. When I saw what a good Spey caster—say, Carl Perry of Portland, Oregon—could do, I became instantly envious. Shamelessly I approached Carl, introduced myself, and began to (as we say) pick his mind.

Carl was kind and generous. He answered my every question with patience. He told me what his personally designed tapers were; I memorized them, on the spot. His knowledge was extensive and exhaustive, I concluded. (If nothing else, I know how to learn.)

Then I brought out my trusty first-generation so-called Spey rod and tried to execute the famous single-Spey from the left bank.

A miserable failure.

Dec Hogan—an old friend—had anchored his driftboat on a bar in the middle of the Skagit River and was instructing a novice in how to catch a steelhead single-handedly in a sweet little gut that ran along the far bank and was unapproachable except from where Dec's boat was parked. To kill a little time while his charge fished, Dec watched me cast. Now I am of a fatherly age in regard to Mr. Hogan and he has always believed I was some sort of expert, having so many years on him in which I've been lucky to fish for steelhead.

To give him full credit, he never cracked a smile during my pathetic performance. He watched, fascinated for a while, with a look of bemused incredulity on his face. Finally I let my tired hands drop to my sides.

"I think," I said lamely, "I need some lessons."

"I'll be happy to give them to you."

But he never did; there wasn't time in his hectic spring schedule of guiding—here, in Oregon, and in Alaska. As for me, I stuck with my old one-handed rod and caught a few fish, as the season droned to an end.

One night at Dec's Rockport-on-the-Skagit camp, I sat around with some young friends of his, waiting for him to return in the dark with his client for a late spaghetti dinner, which was all cooked. The friends were Scott O'Donnell, Brad Adrian (of home-brew fame), and Wayne Cline. Finally Dec and dude drug in.

Dec agreed that a new rod might solve one of my many casting problems. He suggested two possible models, one heavy for winter and spring, and the other light and airy for summer and fall. Then he got busy eating and I, knowing a wife and hot meal were waiting for me forty miles away, piled in my car and blasted off.

The following day I drove away from my place on the Stilly to a favorite downstream pool; the Sauk and Skagit were about to close for the season, which places the time at the very end of April, 1995. In his car at the Whitman Bridge was Wayne Cline from last night. I had never met him before and here he was, seeking me out. He had a spare Spey rod to lend me, he said, plus a sinking line spliced according to Dec Hogan's specifications.

What had I done to deserve this? Nothing, nothing. You can imagine my sense of gratitude. Wayne had come over to help me out. No catch.

So I took his fourteen-foot Spey rod and set out to learn how to cast it. I had read Eric Taverner on Atlantic salmon in the Lonsdale Library Edition over the years and had watched Jim Vincent's video. So armed, I believed I could teach myself Spey casting. And I did. It took me less than a month. To say that I'm proud of my accomplishment is to say the obvious. My point here is, if I can do it, anybody can.

A light-weight Spey rod is a joy to fish with. Both Vincent and Pete Soverel have had considerable experience with them and proclaim a certain thirteen-and-a-half foot rod designed to cast a seven-weight double-taper the best. There is a time to learn from others and a time to muscle it out alone. This was a case for the former. Dec Hogan helped me arrange to fish with this rod and Randy Swisher made it available. Pete and Jim are right. I am married to this sweet stick. (Of course I've been married to other rods in the long-ago.)

Such a rod will cast a floating line with short sinking tip attached a huge distance, I learned, but with a long double-taper floater it is much more pleasing to me to fish with. It casts a ten-weight line sixty to ninety feet easily, and with an eight-weight floating tip section of, say, 15 to 25 feet in length permits a gentle delivery of a fly that either riffles, floats drily, or sinks a bit.

The rod weighs six and a half ounces. This is about the same as the nine-foot Orvis bamboo rod that Jerry Wintle has used, all these thirty-some years, but it is better balanced and much easier to cast with, hour after hour. The bamboo rod's maximum casting distance with an ordinary line is about fifty-five feet. The Spey rod's *starting* distance is about that far, and it is keenly capable of twice that length.

So I stand recanted on the subject. I thought it important to rear right up on my hind legs and say so, especially since this is a book about fishing for steelhead with the floating line. And so I have said it and am done.

Notes on the Fly Plates

Plate One: Dry Flies. Top to bottom, Gray Wulff, Irresistible, Rat-Faced McDougall; White Wulff, Royal Wulff, Black Wulff; Midnight, Spade Dry, Spade Dry Light; Purple Bomber, Orange Bomber (Palmered), Bomber (White-maned).

Plate Two: Spade-type Sub-surface Flies. Comet, Boss, Burlap; Brindle Bug, Spade, Black Spade; Green-butted Spade, Red-butted Spade, Golden Spade (Caddis); Eclipse, Dead Chicken, Red-bodied Spade; Orange and Silver tied Spade-style, Red-tailed Spade, Spade with Pearlescent Butt.

The following plates of flies are all wet, but they were historically fished on floating lines, chiefly because there were no others. Lines of silk would float (for a while) if dressed or "greased"; if not they sank and left for long undressed and wet they quickly rotted. It was not until after World War II that modern sinking lines were manufactured, along with superior floating lines that did not require dressing (and only occasionally cleaning).

Plate Three: Traditional Low-water Wet Flies. Jimmie, Jeannie, Silver Blue; March Brown, Jockie, Bumbec; Black Doctor (reduced), Logie; Crossfield's Brockweir, Crossfield's Black Silk; Gray Heron, Lady Caroline; Akroyd. All tied by John Olshewsky.

Plate Four: Kelson-style Full-dressed Atlantic Salmon Flies. Row one, left, Black Dog; right, Dawson. Row two, left, Sir Herbert; right, Dr. Donaldson. Row three, left, Silver Test; right, Beaconsfield. Row four, Sir Alec; right, Rosy Dawn. Rows one, two and three tied by John Olshewsky. Row four, left, designed by Bob Arnold, tied by Steve Gobin. Row four, right, tied by the late Syd Glasso.

The first four rows are genuine Kelson ties and John is one of the most skillful tiers around. Sir Alec is my effort to honor a friend, Alec Jackson, in the same manner as Poul Jorgenson paid tribute to the actor William Conrad with his special fly, Sir Conrad. The skills necessary to tie this complicated pattern were beyond me, but not Steve Gobin, who did so masterfully.

The Rosy Dawn was tied by Syd Glasso for Rose Jackson and given to her. It is reproduced with her permission. (Since then many tiers have presented a Rosy Dawn to her, and it is becoming a tradition when a tier reaches a certain stage of proficiency.)

Plate Five: Conventional Bucktails, Number One. Timm, Green-butted Skunk; Stewart, Hoyt's Killer; Freight Train, Coal Car; Purple Peril (dressy), Black Woolly Worm; McLeod's Ugly, Killer.

Plate Six: Conventional Bucktails, Number Two. Skykomish Sunrise, Van Luven; Thor, Brad's Brat; Umpqua Special, Max Canyon; Kalama Special, Surgeon General; Orange Steelheader Bucktail.

Note: dressings for most of these flies may be found in a number of books on steelhead fly fishing, so I do not repeat them here.

Plate Seven: Gift Flies, Plate One.

From time to time, anglers I've met on a river have stopped to chat and we have exchanged flies. Or else the flies have come to me in other thoughtful ways. The next two plates are unsolicited contributions to this book by friends and acquaintances. I value them highly.

Top row, left, No Name Blue Fly, Merlin Stidham; dry version of Burlap, Syd Glasso. Note that both of these flies have tippet snells, so that no visible knot attaches the fly to the leader. It is buried under the tiny head. The drawback is that such flies have to be attached by the tippet to the leader and are a bit cumbersome. But, my, how nicely they enter the water and fish. Second row, Golden Spade, originated by Joe Butorac. Joe tied this to represent a caddis with egg sack on the Wenatchee, one year. I was having terrible luck, up until the time he gave me one. An hour later I had beached two fine fish on it, and retired it. But I still tie it and am most grateful. Third row, left, Roderick Haig-Brown's Steelhead Bee, tied by Jerry Wintle and given me in the mid-1960s; right, Preston Jennings's Lord Iris, steelhead version, a gift of Bob Taylor, about the same time. Row four, two versions of Dick Sylbert's Wenatchee River Grey Squirrel and Black Squirrel, typical "fishing" flies and probably ones that themselves caught steelhead. They are good examples of dark flies that may be varied almost endlessly and will consistently catch fish. Fifth row, two versions of Tom Crawford's Bush Baby, one with ordinary gray squirrel and the other with fox squirrel, tied by myself. Notice how Tom lines up the bars on the tail with the bars on the wing. This is a Peter Schwab trick from long ago in California. It still works and produces a more fully winged fly than if it isn't done. Tom likes pearlescent Flashabou in the wing. I don't, but then it is his fly.

Plate Eight: Gift Flies, Plate Two. Top row, three signature flies by Alec Jackson: Spade, a very nice Burlap or Sack Fly, representative of his Softhackled nymph style of tying, and Claret Spade. Second row, left, No Name, Bob Bettzig. Not so well known, Bob (along with Al Knudsen) were strong influences on Walt Johnson's fly tying. Center, the original Skykomish Sunrise, the one on which son George caught his famous three winter steelhead from the Sky, a gift from my mentor Ken, and highly treasured. Right, Wahl Flower, gift of Ralph Wahl and one of his fine Skagit River flies from those great Shangri-La days. Third row, a no-name fly by Eric Balser, which (knowingly or unknowingly) uses golden pheasant crest in about the same manner as the old Irish tyer, Michael Rogan, and is a good steelhead fly, accordingly. Center, Bill McMillan's Winter's Hope, tied by his friend, Scott O'Donnell and a good example of Scott's skills at the vise. Right, Jungle Cock Rock, originated and tied by Writer/Guide Dec Hogan. A good darkish fly for fall, but effective all season. Fourth row, left, Otter Bar Purple, originated and tied by Marty Sherman; center, Floss Fly, originated and tied by the late George Keough. (See below.) Right, one of the Thunder Creek Series, tied by Ed Weinstein in the early 1960s.

Most of the flies and tiers are well known and require no elaboration, but the Keough fly is unique. George tied these on Partridge low-water No. 1 hooks, putting two hooks in a vise made out of a brass door hinge and locked into place with a pair of wing nuts. The hooks were held parallel, but facing away from each other. He then coated the shanks of both hooks with quick-drying epoxy. He wound various fine synthetic flosses from Veniard back and forth over both flies tightly, alternating colors, and let them dry. Then he slit them down the center with a razor blade, making two such flies as the one shown above. Only a few people today know how to do this (or bother to). One is Joe Monda. In the water they make beautiful streamers and tend to fish upside down. (George also invented and patented the epoxy splice many of us use.)

Plate Nine: Akroyd Light, Black Heron; Sweep, Helmsdale; Mignon, Furnace Brown; Sheriff, Beauly Snow Fly; Black King, Akroyd Dark.

Plate Ten: Aglaia, Brora; Candlestick Maker, A Silver Grey Fly; Gled Wing, Miss Grant; Glenn Grant, Mrs. Grant.

The last two plates are tied by myself. They show what a pedestrian tier can do, if he sits down at the bench long enough. This is not false modesty, believe me. I am the originator, by the way, of the Don't Look Back School of Fly Tying. Its precept is, "Finish off that baby quickly and get on to the next." After all, most flies are meant to fish with. They are not intended to hang in a museum. Yet we must strive to do our daily best.

Plate Nine was tied in that awful interval before I got new reading glasses, and the fly heads show it. But they fish well and look good in the water.

Many incorporate "found" feathers from my walks around winter beaches, even though they are well-known patterned flies. Many effective flies can be tied out of cheap or scrounged feathers—seagull, crow, heron, goose, teal, mallard. But you need to have a good eye for what a steelhead fly ought to look like: it is shaggy, streamy, slender, and literally slides through the water.

Most of the patterns in Plate Nine and Ten are traditionally Scottish, some from the River Dee and others incorporating design elements from the River Spey, especially those by the Grant family and recorded by Francis Francis. I would recommend that the steelhead tier who decides to try historical flies in the greased-line mode stick to named patterns and not get too fanciful or "creative" until he has caught a bunch of fish.

Anybody ought to be able to tie flies as good (or as bad) as these in his first season. Some of us, alas, do not get much better with time. Ah, but we still manage to catch fish. And what a joy it is.

In general, the Dee flies have long, flowing wings, while the Speys have short, tented wings of bronze mallard. Both have long streamy heron-like hackles. But not always.

Nothing in steelhead fly fishing is "always."

Previous page, Merlin's Pool

Above: View from Upper Monitor Bridge.

Right: Tumwater Canyon in October.

Below: To the beach. All Wenatchee River, Washington State.

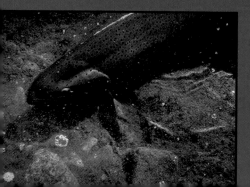

Above: Late winter run from the North Fork Stillaguamish, Washington State. Below: View downstream towards Lower Monitor Bridge on the Wenatchee.

*Charlie Gearheart
fishing Seapost Run.*

Charlie at the Picnic Tables, landing (and keeping) a 17-pound bright hatchery summer run in May. All on the Stillaguamish.

Right: Bright hatchery summer run, Stilly.

Below: Late summer run from the Wenatchee.

Below Right: Close up, hatchery summer run, Wenatchee.

The author and Sam at the bottom of the Camp Pool, Wenatchee.
(photo by John Marshall)

Plate Two

Plate Three

Plate Four

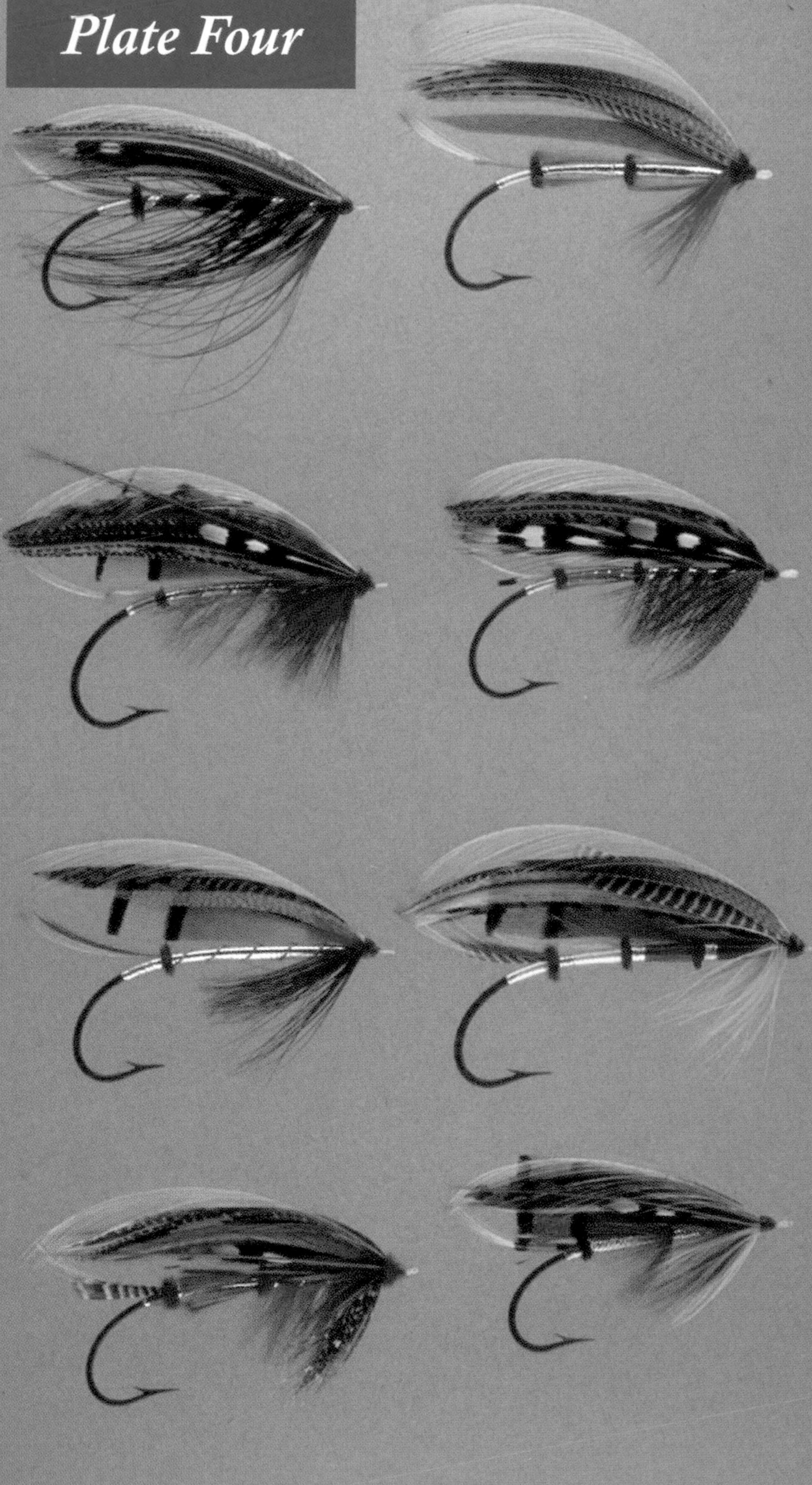

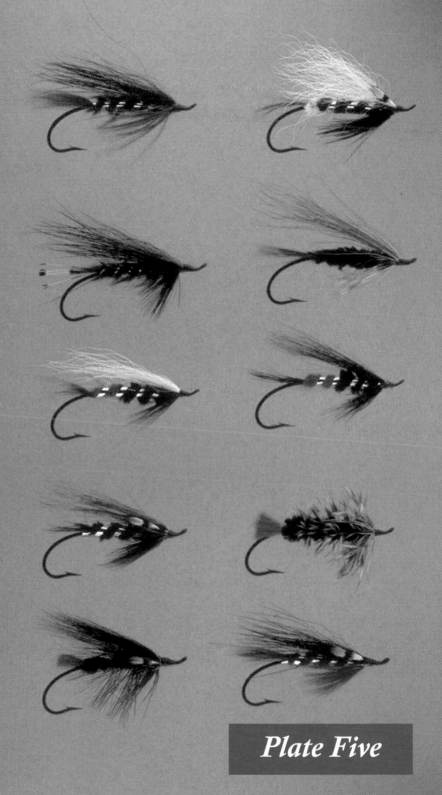

Plate Five